SPORT

PSYCHOLOGY

A SELF-HELP GUIDE

STEPHEN J BULL

The Crowood Press

First published in 1991 by
The Crowood Press Ltd
Ramsbury, Marlborough
Wiltshire SN8 2HR

This impression 2002

British Library Cataloguing-in-Publication Data
A catalogue record for this book is available from the British Library.

ISBN 1 85223 568 3

Dedication

To Junior

Typeset by Falcon Typographic Art Ltd, Edinburgh & London

Printed and bound in Great Britain by Bookcraft, Midsomer Norton

Contents

Acknowledgements

I wish to note many acknowledgements. The first, and most significant, is to my wife Donna, who has demonstrated support, encouragement and patience throughout. My public thanks are extended to the colleagues who contributed a chapter each and hence enabled a vague idea eventually to become a reality. Special thanks are also due to Stuart Biddle and Peter Terry for lively and thought-provoking discussions which have helped frame some of my views as a sport psychologist. And finally, a word of thanks to friends and colleagues at Queen's University and Brighton Polytechnic who have provided practical, scholarly and entertaining feedback since I started working in sport psychology.

The Contributors

Dr Stephen Bull is a senior lecturer at Brighton Polytechnic where he teaches courses in sport psychology, physical education, stress management and the psychological aspects of health and fitness. Before becoming a sport psychologist, he was a PE teacher in England and a recreation officer in Canada. He was a minor counties' rugby player, schoolboy county cricket captain and currently he plays squash, tennis and golf. He is a qualified senior coach with the English National Cricket Association and has also had experience coaching rugby, tennis and basketball. He has been involved in sport psychology consultancy and research since 1984, is co-author of the book *A Mental Game Plan* and is currently Chair of the British Association of Sports Sciences Open Section.

Dr Richard Cox is a lecturer in Movement Studies at the Scottish Centre for Physical Education, Movement and Leisure Studies, Moray House College, Edinburgh. He has worked with the Scottish Women's Bowling Association in preparation for the 1990 Commonwealth Games, and also with the Scottish Netball Association in preparation for the 1987 World Cup.

Dr Graham Jones is a lecturer at Loughborough University. He has written numerous research articles on stress and anxiety in sport. As a sport psychology consultant he currently works with the Great Britain Ice Skating Squad as well as individual performers in a range of other sports. Graham is a member of the Editorial Advisory Board of the *Journal of Sports Sciences* and has recently co-edited a book entitled *Stress and Performance in Sport*.

Dr Larry Leith is an associate professor in the Department of Physical and Health Education at the University of Toronto. He has published over eighty articles on sport psychology topics and has conducted extensive research work in the area of sport aggression.

Dr Stuart Biddle is a lecturer in the School of Education and Associate Director of the Physical Education Association Research Centre at the University of Exeter. Stuart's research interests are in the psychology of success and failure. He has published extensively in sport psychology as well as in physical education and is the author/editor of six books and over fifty research and professional papers. He is currently the British representative on the managing council of the European Federation of Sport Psychology.

Brian Miller is a sport psychologist with vast experience of working with competitive athletes. He spent several years as a consultant at the Australian Institute of Sport in Canberra and has been present at the Olympic Games in an advisory capacity. He now runs his own consultancy in Britain.

Peter Terry is a senior lecturer at the West London Institute of Higher Education. He chaired the Sport Psychology Section of the British Association of Sports Sciences from 1989 to 1990 and is currently a member of the British Olympic Association Psychology Advisory Group. Peter acts as a sport psychology consultant to the Lawn Tennis Association and the British Bobsleigh Association and has helped prepare Olympic and World Championship competitors in many other sports.

John Syer runs a sport psychology and business consultancy with his colleague Christopher Connolly. John is a former international volleyball player and was National Coach for the Scottish Volleyball Association for ten years. He was a staff member of the Findhorn Foundation where he worked with processing techniques, group dynamics and leadership skills. He has special interest and expertise in the area of team building and the development of team spirit.

Misia Gervis is a former gymnast and now a coach for rhythmic gymnasts ranging from club to international standard, and is particularly sensitive to the problems inherent in children's involvement in competitive sport. She is a lecturer in sport psychology at the West London Institute and is a member of the British Olympic Association Psychology Advisory Group.

Dr Adrian Taylor is a senior lecturer at Brighton Polytechnic. He has acted as player, coach, official and administrator in numerous sports including soccer, rugby, basketball, track and field, and orienteering. Professionally, Adrian taught health and physical education for six years in schools before completing a doctorate in exercise science at the University of Toronto.

CHAPTER ONE

Introduction to Sport Psychology

Dr Stephen J. Bull

The healthy mind in a healthy body philosophy dates back as far as the ancient Chinese and Greek civilizations. However, it is only in recent years that the discipline, now known as sport psychology, has become recognized and acknowledged as a major component in the science of sport performance.

Sport psychology has developed and grown significantly in the past two decades. Media interest continues to increase, and the scientific body of knowledge relating to the area has become so large that different branches of the subject have begun to emerge. In its widest sense sport psychology encompasses the psychological aspects of competitive sport, exercise, fitness, leisure and motor skill development. Many textbooks and scholarly journals exist to demonstrate the extent of research and educational work in these areas. This book, however, does not attempt to cover all aspects of sport psychology. Instead, it focuses specifically on factors relating closely to behaviour and performance in competitive sport. Each chapter addresses a different topic and is written with practical examples. This will aid your understanding and enable you to improve either your own performance, or that of others.

Historical Development of Sport Psychology

In 1895 George Fitz carried out an experiment on reaction time which is recognized as one of the earliest investigations examining psychological processes and sport performance. About the same time Norman Triplett studied the relationship between the presence of other competitors and performance in cycle racing. He discovered that cycling times were faster against competitors than when cycling alone. He thus launched an area of research which is still investigated today – the influence of rival athletes in sport. Why do some athletes rise to the

The healthy mind in a healthy body philosophy dates back as far as the ancient Chinese and Greek civilizations.

occasion when performing in front of a crowd, under pressure, whereas others seem to fall apart?

To try and answer such questions, Coleman Griffith established the very first sport psychology research laboratory in 1925. It was situated at the University of Illinois in America. Soon afterwards laboratories of a similar nature were set up in Berlin and Leningrad. In 1965 the first convention of the International Congress of Sport Psychology took place in Rome. Similar conventions have continued to occur at regular intervals since then, with the most recent being hosted by Singapore in the summer of 1989.

Today, there are hundreds of sport psychologists working throughout the world. Many teach students in universities and colleges, and conduct research in a constant effort to improve our understanding of the psychological processes which influence behaviour and performance in sport and physical activity. This book is a practical guide which examines some of these factors, and suggests ways in which you can improve your understanding of sport psychology. You will then be able to use this knowledge to enhance the role that you play in sport, whether it be as a player, coach, referee or parent.

The Content of this Book

In editing this book I have recruited the assistance of several leading international sport psychologists who have expertise and specialized knowledge in different areas within the psychology of competitive sport. Together, they possess a wealth of academic and practical experience which they have obviously drawn upon in preparing their contributions to the book.

Chapter 2 is an examination of one of the most fundamental elements of any aspect of human behaviour – motivation. It explains the complexities of human motivation and analyses how we can increase motivation by a variety of means. There are plenty of exercises for you to complete as you read the chapter, and a number of very important suggestions if you are a coach who wishes to maintain or promote the motivation of your athletes. The chapter concludes with a section on goal setting which is relevant to motivation and performance in any sporting context and should be read carefully by both athletes and coaches alike.

Chapter 3 examines the area of stress and anxiety. After defining the subject, it describes competitive anxiety as a personality dimension, competitive anxiety and sports performance, and suggests how you can maintain psychological control under competitive stress. The chapter includes anxiety questionnaires which you can do yourself, as a means of assessing your own personal predisposition to stress and anxiety. This chapter is a must for anyone who tends to suffer from pre-performance tension and nerves.

Chapter 4 takes a look at aggression and the different ways of defining the subject before assessing its causes. It also analyses how these causes can be modified or adapted to reduce unacceptable aggressive responses. The chapter contains a wealth of implications, and provides a number of practical techniques for athletes and coaches.

Chapter 5 examines the ways in which sports performers interpret success and failure. It analyses the reasons competitors give for their performance results, and their reactions to them. This is an important area as it relates very closely to future levels of motivation following satisfying and dissatisfying sporting performances.

The sixth chapter focuses on mental preparation for competition, and covers six important elements of mental preparation – centering, visualization, performance segmenting, pre-event focusing, energizing, and goal setting. Each element will benefit competitive athletes of all standards, and in all sports. Coaches will also find the chapter useful for encouraging their athletes to adopt the techniques as part of their overall training programme. There are practical exercises which encourage you to experiment with the techniques, as well as plenty of illustrations from world-class athletes who have used the techniques successfully.

In Chapter 7 the psychology of the coach–athlete relationship is dealt with, including the concept of coaching and various coaching styles. The interaction theory of coaching is also explained, and research findings relating to the coaching preferences of athletes are discussed. The chapter concludes with a very useful practical section outlining a number of guidelines for successful coaching, including effective communication and leadership behaviour.

Chapter 8 examines the area of team building, outlining the role a coach can play in this process by suggesting various practical techniques which facilitate the development of team spirit. Advice on how to conduct team meetings, how to deal with individuals and the best ways to give feedback are integral parts of the chapter. This is an ideal section for any coach or group leader wishing to improve the communication between members of a sports group.

The ninth chapter tackles the controversial area of children in sport. Competitive sport is examined from the child's point of view, and as a follow-up ways of helping children enjoy participating in sport more, and the reduction of competitive stress are then discussed. There is an important section for parents, as well as an analysis of the coach–parent relationship. This chapter is ideal for anyone involved in organizing, teaching, or coaching children's and/or youth sports.

Chapter 10 deals with burnout and includes a number of interesting exercises giving you an indication of your rating on the burnout scale. How burnout develops, what the symptoms may be, and how to avoid or recover from burnout are all discussed. The chapter will also be of great interest to individuals feeling stressed and dissatisfied in other aspects of their life.

In Chapter 11 the role of the sport psychologist is examined, along with performance enhancement training, lifestyle management, and coach education. A number of ethical considerations are reviewed, and a descriptive framework to illustrate how a practising sport psychologist operates is presented.

In the final chapter a number of conclusions and recommendations are provided, with various recommendations for athletes, coaches, referees, parents, and potential sport psychologists.

As you begin to read each chapter, you will notice that there are a number of exercises for you to complete as you progress. It is a good idea, therefore, to keep a notebook and pen at your side. It would be worth labelling this as your 'Sport psychology workbook' which you could keep for future reference.

And finally, you will note that I have avoided providing a definition of sport psychology. In fact as you progress through the book you will probably develop your own definition. Whatever that definition becomes, it will undoubtedly be more than just 'psyching up athletes' or 'helping athletes handle the pressure of competition'. You will find that there is so much more to sport psychology than pre-match pep talks.

CHAPTER TWO

Motivation

Dr Richard Cox

If one subject matter could be said to pervade and underpin every other identified in this book it is motivation. Motivation, of one kind or another, is responsible for most of our thoughts, emotions, and deeds. So, some people are motivated to take up sport, and some to make enormous sacrifices in the pursuit of fame and glory. In fact nothing that happens in sport is devoid of motivation on the part of individuals. It therefore makes sense for those concerned with sport, be they athletes, coaches, administrators, officials, ardent fans or occasional spectators, to understand and appreciate something about the concept of motivation.

Intrinsic and Extrinsic Motivation

Many of those who have spoken or written about this subject refer to 'intrinsic' and 'extrinsic' motivation. Intrinsic motivation is said to come from within the person, and extrinsic motivation from the surrounding environment. The problem with this approach is that any motivation described as intrinsic stops there, and fails to dig deeper. An example would be the boxer who is described as being 'hungry for success'. He is said to be 'intrinsically motivated', and that is usually sufficient to satisfy those who wish to understand why he fights. But why is he 'hungry'? Why isn't his brother, who comes from the same background, equally hungry for success? Conversely, why does a world champion and multi-millionaire, who cannot be hungry in any sense of the word, continue to fight even after he has been advised by doctors not to do so?

If intrinsic motivation means anything then why do people who have no hope of winning run themselves to exhaustion, and even death, in marathon races? It cannot be because they are intrinsically motivated because, inside, these people must be feeling terrible with their bodies screaming at them to stop. The truth of the matter is human motivation is extremely complex both to account for and to understand. Even accounting for one's own motivation is difficult enough, for although we can always give good reasons for why we do the things we do, it is far harder to identify the real reasons. (If it were otherwise psychiatrists would be largely redundant.) Now think how much harder it is to account for someone else's motivation, and yet that is precisely what coaches, for instance, are attempting to do for their athletes throughout most of their involvement with them.

Exercise 1

Try to identify two of the real reasons for your own involvement in sport. Be specific and try to go beyond the single, emotional statement such as 'I enjoy it' or 'It gives me a buzz'. These statements do no more than beg the questions 'why do you enjoy it', 'what is there about the sport to enjoy', and 'why might someone else not enjoy it?'.

1 _____

2 _____

Exercise 2

Now do the same for the person closest to you in sport.

1. _____

2. _____

The only definite intrinsic motivators which are beyond question or dispute are hunger and thirst. The motivation to survive is paramount and this is evidenced by the incredible lengths humans will go to find food and water. Many will argue that the sex drive is the third major intrinsic motivation, and for psychoanalysts such as Freud it was, and remains, the great source of all human motivation. Nevertheless, the sex drive cannot be on the same level as hunger and thirst for many people choose to live celibate lives. No such choice is available as regards hunger and thirst if the individual wishes to survive.

Primary and Secondary Motivation

In terms of trying to understand and account for motivation in sport, it is perhaps more helpful to think in terms of primary and secondary sources of motivation. Primary motivation is derived from the activity itself. Thus, hitting the ball accurately and with control in squash and tennis provides primary motivation because hitting the ball is not dependent on another person at the point of impact. Most top class squash players, for instance, practise on their own for up to two hours every day. Whilst their motivation for doing so may well be deferred in that such practice is only a means to an end (winning an important match or tournament), nevertheless many derive considerable satisfaction from solo practice for its own sake.

Golf provides a better example because, where rules allow, people of all ages can be seen playing on their own. Who would argue with someone who says they play golf because of the challenge the game itself provides? They do not have to beat anyone to sustain motivation, and they indeed are the reason why most driving ranges make a profit. The long distance runner, solo yachtsman and mountain climber provide perhaps even more obvious examples. The challenges these activities offer are enough to account for why large numbers of people take part in them.

The definition of secondary motivation follows almost as a straightforward deduction from that of primary motivation. That is to say any forms of influence, except those associated directly with engaging in the activity itself, are secondary sources of motivation. Thus, a coach is a source of secondary motivation, as are parents, peers, audiences, prizes, badges, certificates, trophies, medals and money. Being part of a team or squad also provides secondary motivation through the attention and companionship gained from the presence of others. Theoretically, it should be easy to distinguish between primary and secondary sources of motivation for one need ask but one question which is, 'when all obvious sources of secondary motivation are removed, does the person concerned continue with the activity?' It sounds straightforward but, in practice, this question is nigh on impossible to answer because of our ability to plan for the future on the one hand, and to harbour ulterior motives for behaviour on the other. Nevertheless, it is a question worth asking, particularly by coaches of their athletes, because, if nothing else, it helps to discover something about athletes' level of commitment to their sport.

Exercise 3

Think about the following examples and decide which are more likely to be primary sources of motivation and which are secondary:

Examples

	Primary		Secondary
1. Financial bonus to a professional footballer.		1	
2. The feeling of effortlessness as the sprinter 'eats up' the track.		2	
3. Being awarded an Olympic gold medal.		3	
4. Completing a triple axel (ice skating) successfully.		4	
5. Hitting the nick (squash) with a 'kill' drive.		5	
6. Scoring a try in rugby.		6	
7. Beating the Americans in the Ryder Cup (for European golfers).		7	
8. Sailing the Atlantic Ocean single-handed.		8	
9. Winning the Men's Singles Championship at Wimbledon.		9	
10. Being appointed captain of the swimming club.		10	

Positive and Negative Motivation

The complexity of human motivation is emphasized by the fact that both primary and secondary sources of motivation can be either *positive* or *negative*. Often they are both, though never at the same time. An example of a primary source that can be both positive and negative in succession is the sun. The typical British sunbather revels in the warm, Mediterranean sunshine on the first day of a holiday but the next day, with burnt skin, sits covered up in the shade praying for cloud.

In sport an athlete can either be performing well (primary positive) or performing badly (primary negative). By continuing to perform badly for a long period the motivation for wanting to continue in that sport will begin to diminish, and eventually might cause the athlete to give it up. Thus, a decision to retire from a particular sport might be a reflection of an imbalance that has built up between primary positive and primary negative motivation. In other words, the athlete no longer derives sufficient satisfaction from participating in the activity to want to continue.

In a similar way, an audience (secondary) can either be biased for (positive) or against (negative) a player or team, and the power of their influence can be identified partly in the advantages playing at home usually affords. Of course, why this should be is a fascinating question in itself, and yet how many coaches and players in professional football, for instance, bother to raise it? Given that the away team has the same number of players as the home team, that the two goal areas are the same size, the referee and linesmen are supposedly neutral, and the pitch is virtually a standard size, there is no obvious reason why playing away should be a disadvantage. Obviously a partisan crowd can upset some players, and this is one reason why sport psychologists are now using pre-recorded audience noises at practice venues to simulate the competition environment. But the home crowd does not always support the home team, and it wouldn't be the first time a professional footballer has asked for a transfer in order to escape from a vociferous home crowd that 'has it in for him' (secondary negative).

Of course, using such terms as 'having it in for someone', 'failure', 'success', 'satisfaction', 'playing well' and 'performing badly', does little towards helping us understand the concept of motivation. People are motivated, either positively or negatively, by the consequences of their own behaviour (thoughts, feelings and actions). So, if every time a particular footballer receives the ball he gets verbal abuse from a section of the crowd because they 'have it in for him', then it would be hardly surprising if he no longer wanted the ball. Similarly, being labelled a 'failure' in sport is the end result of any number of incidences in which the consequences of the behaviour of the individual concerned have been perceived negatively by others in some way. Golfers may label themselves a 'failure' if they cannot hit the golf ball down the fairway or, worse still, cannot hit it at all. If the number of shots hit into the rough, out of bounds, or missed altogether heavily outweighs the number of 'good' shots then such players may conclude that they are 'no good at golf'.

On the positive side 'success', 'satisfaction' and 'playing well' are terms that are used to reflect consequences of behaviour that are perceived positively. Thus, the goalkeeper who makes a series of brilliant saves, the striker who scores a winning goal, and the defender who makes a match-saving tackle will all be rewarded in some way by the consequences of their efforts. They are rewarded instantly by their actions in keeping the ball out of the goal, seeing the ball enter the goal, and stopping an opponent

*If one subject matter could be said to pervade and underpin
every other identified in this book it is motivation.*

from shooting for goal. They are rewarded immediately after by the congratulations of their team-mates and acclaim from the crowd, and rewarded again later when they read of their play in the newspapers. The effect of all this on the individuals concerned is that they 'enjoy playing', 'think positively' about themselves, and 'look forward' to the next game.

The consequences of taking part in sport are almost always either rewarding or punishing in the extreme. It is difficult, if not impossible, to be emotionally neutral about sport even when, for example, the professional footballer is playing his fiftieth match of the season. He may be described as 'simply going through the motions', but inwardly he may well experience the full range of emotions as he does something well one minute and makes a costly mistake the next. His emotional feelings are the end results of the consequences of what he does during the match, minute by minute.

Figure 1 summarizes the points made so far. The relationships between performance and outcome are complex in terms of overall effect. (This point is returned to later in this chapter under the heading 'Goal-Setting.')

Feedback

The consequences of our own behaviour become known to us through what is called 'feedback'. Like motivation, feedback can be divided between primary and secondary sources. Primary sources of feedback are an integral part of everything we do. Thus, as I am writing these very words I am receiving visual primary feedback about the style and legibility of my writing, and the meaning of the words. I am also receiving auditory primary feedback from the noise my pen makes on the paper, and through the muscles (kinaesthetic) and joints (proprioceptive) of my writing hand, wrist and arm as I write. The latter two derive from changes in tension in the muscles, and changes in the position of my hand and arm as it moves across the page and back again. Simultaneously, I am also receiving primary feedback from my body in terms of its position on and contact with the chair, from the soles of my feet through their contact with the carpet, from my neck and lower back because I am sitting in a stooped position and they are beginning to ache, and from my stomach because it is quite a while since I ate.

Yet, while primary feedback always occurs people are not always conscious of it. For instance, the only feedback I am

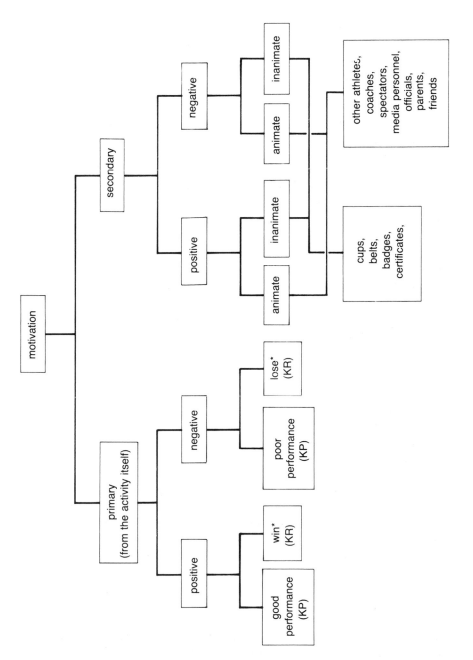

Fig 1   Sources of human motivation.

noticing as I write is the sense and flow of each sentence because they are the most important things to me at this moment. Everything else is temporarily relegated to the background and to my subconscious. This highlights the fact that we selectively attend to things that are important to us and we do so one at a time.

Exercise 4

Pause for a moment and try to identify:

1. The focus of your immediate attention _____
2. What you were attending to before that _____

Now focus on:

1. The *auditory* feedback you are receiving – from whom or what is it coming, and from which direction? _____
   _____
2. The *kinaesthetic* feedback you are receiving through the major muscle groups in your body; which are most tense?
   _____
   the most relaxed? _____
   the most painful (if at all)? _____
3. The *tactile* feedback you are receiving through the various points of contact your body has with objects around you – the chair, floor etc. _____
   _____

Secondary sources of feedback augment, or add to, the information we gain from primary sources. Thus, coaches are a source of secondary feedback in that they comment (verbal) on our performances which we receive through our ears (auditory); they might show us what we did wrong by providing a demonstration (visual), or they might guide our racket arm, in tennis for example, through a movement that did not register with the player who was concentrating on the ball. To guide our racket arm in this way (manual guidance) they must touch us (tactile), which augments the kinaesthetic and proprioceptive (primary) feedback we received from our racket arm when we did the movement unaided.

When writing about sport it is commonplace to describe feedback in terms of 'knowledge of performance' (K.P.) and 'knowledge of results' (K.R.). Knowledge of performance is intrinsic to the task and about which we receive primary feedback through our movements. **Figure 2** makes these points clearer. So, for instance, in attempting a 3 ft (0.9m) putt the golfer gains primary

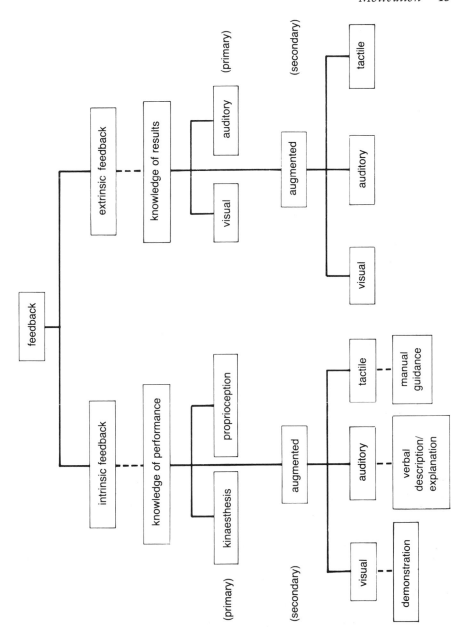

Fig 2   Sources of feedback.

knowledge of performance through kinaesthetic and proprioceptive feedback, i.e. how hard and smoothly the ball is hit, and gains primary knowledge of results through seeing (visual) the outcome of the attempt and through hearing (auditory) the club striking the ball.

Knowledge of results can be augmented, for instance, by the instant, computerized display of the results of a swimming race or the huge television screens now used at major athletics competitions. These provide visual feedback, just as the loudspeaker system provides auditory feedback, and the shaking of one's hand or pat on the back provides tactile feedback.

What has been explained so far can now be represented diagrammatically, as shown in **Figure 3**, with the sequence of events being most important.

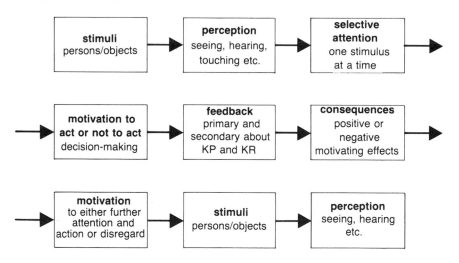

Fig 3   The relationship between action, feedback and motivation.

Two observations on this figure are worth making. First, the sequence of events is represented linearly but it could just as easily be shown as a circular loop. Second, and more important for present purposes, it reveals a relationship between motivation and feedback that is crucial to an understanding of human behaviour. We are motivated to do things and, having done them, receive feedback from a number of sources which we interpret either positively or negatively. This interpretation, in turn, affects our motivation to do them again, either immediately or at some future time. Teaching a child to swim provides a good example. Initially, the parent or coach engages the child in a variety of games and exercises, the intention presumably being to develop confidence in the water. The child receives positive feedback (primary) from the water in that it provides support and is usually warm (anyone attempting to teach a child to swim in the North Sea is going to have a hard time!). The child also receives positive feedback (secondary) from the reactions of the parent or coach, who will be encouraging and conveying to the child that they are pleased with their efforts. But sometimes things go wrong. For instance, the child might be invited to put his face under water which will have to be done sooner or later for a successful swim. And of course it also develops confidence. But, instead of holding breath the child breathes in. The immediate consequences (primary negative) are disastrous, and the coach now has a difficult task in pacifying the child and restoring confidence. In fact there are many adults who are terrified of water because of such a traumatic incident (primary negative) that happened when a child.

This example brings into question a cherished belief in coaching sport that simply by repeating an action over and over again the athlete automatically 'grooves it in'. This may well happen, but not if the consequences of each repetition are negative. Coaches, teachers and parents would do well to ask themselves the following question beforehand, 'If I ask my athlete/pupil/offspring to do something, what are the most likely consequences?'

This is where empathy and experience can play an important part in the selection of exercises, routines, simulated movements and conditioned games (depending on the sport) by the person in charge. Choosing the most appropriate practices and organizing them to maximize effectiveness is one of the most difficult and skilful tasks demanded of the coach or teacher. For information, some principles of practice are listed in **Figure 5**, and particular attention should be paid to those numbered 7 and 8. This is because they focus on primary sources of feedback. To do this is to develop the learner's powers of self-assessment which are crucial to progress and development.

Most coaches believe they know the best way to improve performance and, in the realms of physical fitness and training methods for instance, they are backed up by a wealth of scientific information. But the truth of the matter is no one knows for certain the best way to bring an athlete to peak physical fitness at a given time. Coaches may claim they know this, but the balance between the genetic endowment of an individual and the thousands of events that have shaped character, attitudes and beliefs is so fine and complex that, at best, such claims should only be made in terms of probability, and tentatively so at that.

Initial motivation

What has not yet been accounted for in the relationship between motivation and feedback is the initial motivation of people wanting to try something they have never tried before. The neophyte cannot be motivated by primary sources until an activity has been tried. Thus, for instance, the officials of the track and field athletics club who organize an open day for youngsters to 'come and try athletics' will do well to remember that most of those who attend are there because of secondary motivators. The most likely sources of these secondary motivators are parents and peer groups, with television influence not far behind. Whether or not any of them want to return to the club will be determined by their experiences (primary) of track and field athletics on the day.

Now, herein lies a potential problem because many concerned with athletics as a competitive sport, well-meaning though they may be, are either reluctant or unable to think beyond the conventional distances and equipment for competing. Thus, the shortest distance they would ask anyone to sprint is either 80 or 100m; they never involve more than four people in a relay race; hurdles have to be of a certain height, number and distance apart; and the smallest throwing implements they offer are typically those used by adult ladies in international competition. (Why a 12 year old should be asked to throw the same size javelin as Fatima Whitbread, or the same size discus as the East German world champion is beyond comprehension.) What is predictable is that if complete beginners are introduced to track and field athletics in this way then most children will receive primary, negative feedback from their efforts. Furthermore, only those who 'win' and receive congratulations from officials, parents and peers are likely to be tempted back.

Of course, if the aim of the open day is to 'spot talent' then the officials of the club will not mind if only the 'winners' return. Indeed, it may be their policy to invite only the 'winners' to return. Sadly, such a policy would almost certainly reject many who have the potential to do well later on, and would contribute little to raising the status of track and field athletics in the country as a whole. There are many ways in which this problem could be tackled. One would be to record everything everyone does on the day. Thus, for instance, every competitor would attempt, say, five events and be given either a time or distance for their performances in each. These times and distances would be recorded on a certificate in the youngster's name and handed out at the end of the day's proceedings. A good choice of events would be as follows:

1.   40m sprint.
2.   40m hurdles – three hurdles spaced 5m apart, and 2 ft in height, with the weights positioned to offer the least resistance possible.
3.   400m 'distance' race – *not* to be run in lanes.
4.   Long-jump – four attempts each from a maximum run-up of 15m. All four jumps to be measured from wherever take-off occurs.
5.   Throwing a cricket ball or a baseball – four attempts from a maximum run-up of 5m. All four to be measured from last point of contact before throwing.

Exercise 5

1.   Which activities or practices in your sport are usually chosen for complete beginners?

   1 _____

   2 _____

   3 _____

2.   How do these activities or practices allow complete beginners to be successful?

   1. _____

   2. _____

   3. _____

3.   Could these activities or practices be improved in any way? (e.g. modifying size of equipment, number of participants, time, distance, playing area).

   1. _____

   2. _____

   3. _____

Ideally, this programme for children would not end here. As the results from the running events come in someone would be grading them into teams of 10 of approximately equal merit. The children would then be moved onto a programme of team relays, the scope for which at an athletics stadium is virtually limitless. For instance, instead of a 4 × 100m relay, the children would race in a 10 × 40m relay, once on the flat and again over two hurdles each. When the inner field area and other forms of locomotion such as hopping, skipping, jumping and leap-frogging are taken into consideration, it is not difficult to envisage how children could receive positive primary feedback from their introduction to track and field athletics. In turn, this raises the probability of their wanting to return to the stadium for a second time.

This example raises the question of how much 'success' (the combination of primary and secondary feedback) an individual requires in order to sustain motivation at an optimal level. With beginners the answer is 'as much and as often as possible', with the majority coming from the primary source, the activity itself. Thus, it is crucial that the person in charge selects practices that are known to appeal to beginners and allow for 'success' to be experienced relatively frequently while at the same time providing opportunity for basic competencies to be developed. It is this kind of thinking that has led to the development of 'mini' games in rugby, soccer, tennis, volleyball, etc.

Beginners also thrive on positive feedback from secondary sources, and particularly from important adults. Thus, parents, teachers and coaches should be careful as to what they say to beginners and how they say it. (This point is developed more fully in the section entitled 'Verbal Feedback'.) Criticism and, even worse sarcasm, have negative effects on the vast majority of people, and motivate them to escape from the source and its causes. This means that, for beginners in a sport, the majority are likely to give it up. The person in charge should choose words (verbal feedback) very carefully.

Providing the most appropriate feedback for beginners in sport suggests that the ideal coaching situation is one coach to every pupil. Tennis, squash and ice-skating are sports in which this arrangement is commonplace. It allows the coach the opportunity to observe everything the pupil does and to adjust the practices and give feedback at precisely the right moment. The moment a second pupil is introduced the coach's attention is divided and the problem of timing feedback becomes more difficult. It is mainly for this reason that in Principles of Practice (see **Figure 4**), numbers 7 and 8, are so important.

1. All practices should be chosen as a result of assessment.
2. All practices should be chosen to suit the learners' present level of skill.
3. All practices should be introduced with clear objectives.
4. Objectives for any practice should be stated in order of priority.
5. Objectives for any practice must be communicated clearly to the learners before they begin to practise.
6. The increment in the degree of difficulty between any two progressively related practices should be as small as possible.
7. All practices should be designed to develop learners' awareness of their own performances and outcomes.
8. Whenever possible, practices should be designed to bring about the desired effect *in themselves* and thereby reduce the amount of verbal feedback to a minimum.
9. All practices should reflect in a meaningful way what is required in the 'whole' skill or situation.
10. Sufficient time should be allowed for learners to adapt to the demands of the practice.
11. Learners should be given a rest from practice the moment their performance begins to deteriorate. However, the practice should be returned to subsequently, perhaps many times.
12. All feedback provided by the teacher/coach should be in keeping with the objectives stated for the practice.
13. Practice reinforces ideas.
14. Only *perfect* practice eventually gives *perfect* results.

Fig 4   Principles of practice.

Once beginners have enjoyed the taste of success on more than one occasion, so the frequency of 'success' can be reduced without reducing motivation. It must be borne in mind however, that the nature of success will change as the beginner progresses. Initially, the latter will be content with demonstrating skills occasionally, whereas the experienced competitor will take these for granted and, indeed, may judge success solely in terms of, for instance, national ranking at the end of a season. At the top end an Olympic champion may go more than a year without any obvious success while preparing for a major competition. However, providing success is achieved by the competitor's own standards in that competition, motivation for participating in the sport will continue undiminished. Such an athlete was Lasse Viren, the Finnish middle distance runner. He won the Olympic gold medals for 5,000m and 10,000m in 1972, did nothing of any note for the next four years, but repeated his gold medal winning achievements in the same two events in Montreal, 1976. He had had very little obvious success for four years, but because of the way he had set his goals it did not affect his motivation.

Verbal Feedback

Coaches, teachers and parents all provide secondary feedback to their charges of one kind or another. In sport the coach is usually the main source of secondary feedback, and this is provided mainly through language (verbal feedback). The quality and quantity of verbal feedback given to learners depends largely upon three factors: (i) the coach's knowledge of the sport, (ii) the latter's powers of observation and analysis, and (iii) the coach's degree of sensitivity and tact.

Verbal feedback can take many forms, each of which has quite predictable effects upon the majority of learners. This point is perhaps best illustrated by example in the form of the following four questions which coaches might ask themselves.

1.   Are the majority of feedback statements I make to my athletes *value* statements? That is, do I say such things as 'well done', 'good shot', 'that's great', more than any other type of statement?
2.   When I give corrective feedback, such as 'you failed to keep your wrist cocked' or 'your feet were in the wrong position', is it usually phrased negatively, as are these examples, rather than positively?
3.   When coaching more than one athlete at a time do I usually give feedback to an individual so that others can hear what I am saying?
4.   Do I usually give feedback to my athletes whilst they are actually working and practising?

Assuming you as a coach answer these questions definitively and in the affirmative, then you would do well to review your typical verbal behaviour for the following reasons. First, if the majority of feedback statements are value statements only, then the coach is providing what might be termed 'fuzzy feedback'. What does 'well done' or 'good shot' mean to the learner? Does the latter know why it was well done, or why it was a good shot and how it was produced? Would the learner be able to reproduce the shot from this kind of feedback? The answer is probably not, and although feedback of this kind can motivate beginners initially it soon becomes ineffective and, if persisted with, can actually become counter-productive. Second, if corrective feedback (this is feedback that contains information) is typically negative in kind then it is likely to inhibit the majority of pupils and make them over anxious to please. This, in turn, can lead to increased muscle tension which is seldom helpful to performance. Third, these problems are likely to be made worse if the coach gives negative feedback and others hear what the individual concerned is doing wrong. And finally, if the coach insists on giving feedback while the pupil is in the process of practising then it is more likely to prove a source of distraction than encouragement – imagine a golf coach giving feedback during the pupil's swing or a diving coach shouting something just as the pupil begins movement on the 10m board.

In general, the negative effects described above are worse for beginners than for experienced athletes. But for all athletes it is better to . . .

1.   Give praise (value laden feedback) only when athletes understand clearly the reasons for it.
2.   Phrase corrective feedback in the positive, such as 'try to do this' rather than 'don't do that.'
3.   Impart criticism privately so that athletes do not suffer the added embarrassment of having their 'weaknesses' exposed to others.
4.   Give feedback immediately after performance, rather than during it or some time after it has been completed.

Figure 5 provides an illustrated summary of the types of verbal feedback typically given to athletes. Two details in this figure now need to be mentioned. The first is the division between subject matter and role. Most feedback in sport concerns athletic performance – how well one played, or ran, or swam, etc. Feedback about role is less common because it refers to how well athletes carry out the coach's instructions. An example would be, 'You carried out the strategy I planned for you exactly; thank you and well done'. This is a positive value statement about role, and it could quite legitimately be followed up with, 'Now all we have to do is get the strategy right and we might start winning!' Obviously, this would be an extreme example but it highlights the difference between role and performance.

The second detail to mention concerns neutral statements. Neutral statements are statements of fact and contain neither value judgements nor corrective information. An example would be, 'I see you are wearing your club tracksuit today.' Now, whilst this is a statement of fact the effect upon the individual to whom

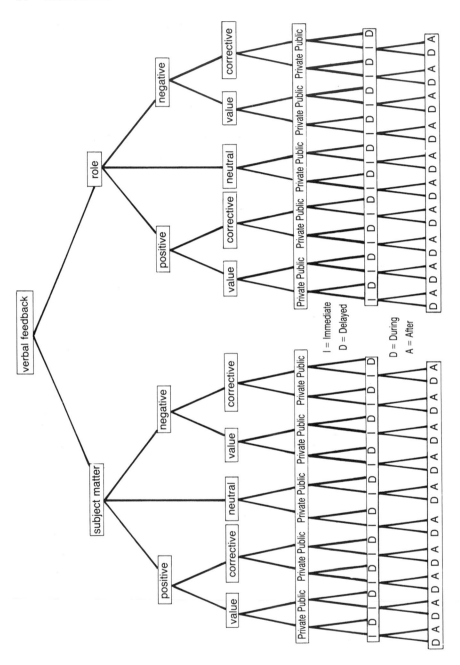

Fig 5   *Types of verbal feedback.*

it is directed is anything but neutral. This is because we believe everyone has a motive for anything they say and, as a consequence, most individuals will respond to neutral statements as though they were questions. Thus 'I see you are wearing your club track suit today' is interpreted by the recipient as 'Why are you wearing your club tracksuit today?' and the latter feels compelled to justify the choice of tracksuit. This is why developing the skill of making neutral statements is a useful ploy because it often provides information without having to ask for it. It is not to be overdone, however, for neutral statements have a tendency to put people on their guard and suspect ulterior motives.

Goal-Setting

Everyone in sport has a goal of some kind. It may be set by themselves or for them by a coach. Setting goals is vitally important if motivation is to be sustained or increased. All too often, however, goals are set inappropriately and serve only to create negative motivation which reduces the desire to continue. This is why setting goals appropriately is a high level skill and is one feature of coaching that distinguishes the effective coaches from their lesser counterparts. The novice coach is far more likely to impose goals on athletes rather than negotiate them with each individual. Moreover, the new coach is far more likely to set a single goal and identify it in terms of winning and losing rather than performance. In other words, the novice is more likely to set goals which are not under the direct control of the athletes.

One often quoted American football coach is reported to have told his athletes that, 'Winning is not a matter of life or death; it's far more important than that.' These are fine words which lead one to conclude that he must have been an inspirational coach. The problem is, however, that winning a competition is not under the direct control of the players. That coach's players might have played the best football of their careers and yet been beaten. Would that mean they had failed? Winning is important in competitive sport, and even more so for professionals as their livelihood depends upon it. But winning is the outcome of performance and is not under the direct control of anyone. The coach who tells athletes to 'get out there and win, I don't care how you do it,' is bound to affect their motivation adversely sooner or later. In so far as an athlete, or team, can win and play well, win and play badly, lose and play well, or lose and play badly, it makes sense to evaluate athletes in terms of performance rather than outcome. Thus, goals negotiated in terms of skills, tactics, strategies, thought content, and application are more likely to prove positively motivating in the long run than winning or losing because they can be controlled by the athletes concerned.

The effective coach, therefore, is more likely to:

1.   Negotiate goals with athletes.
2.   Negotiate several goals at more than one level.
3.   Negotiate goals in terms of performance rather than outcome.

The term negotiate is used frequently to identify the process of goal-setting. If a coach tells athletes what goals to pursue then, even if they are set in terms of performance, they will still create problems. This is because the athletes will start performing for the person in charge rather than for themselves which, in turn, provides a fertile breeding ground for the universal dread among athletes – 'fear of failure.' This fear is developed from falling short of other people's expectations and is the main reason why so many athletes are now seeking psychological help or even giving up sport altogether. Failing in other people's eyes is one of the most negative experiences of all.

When goals are negotiated between coach and athlete the latter is more committed to them. It is like signing a contract, the details of which are set out clearly for both parties to discuss. The experienced coach has a good idea of what athletes are capable of, and is therefore able to help them set realistic goals. The coach would probably begin the process of negotiating goals with a question, something along the following lines (the example given is of a track coach to a top male 800m runner):

'Well, given what you did in your last race, and your current form, how do you think you are likely to fare in this week's race?'

The first question is always a general one. If the athlete replies in terms of winning then it becomes necessary to guide the athlete towards performance goals. The effective coach will negotiate goals at more than one level as this helps both parties evaluate performance in greater detail than is allowed by a single goal. Thus, the next question might be, 'What should you manage to achieve if everything goes according to plan?'

A sophisticated answer in terms of performance goals might be as follows:

'I should manage 54 seconds for the first 400m because I intend going off fast and I'd like to be leading when we break from the lanes. That

way I can control the pace. If anyone wants to run faster than that then I'll be on his shoulder down the first back straight. If not, I'm taking the race on myself as my best chance of a good result is to run some of the speed out of the other guy's legs. After the bell I should be able to keep the same speed going until the last 200m. From then on I intend concentrating on staying relaxed and maintaining good form to the end. That way I should manage between 1 min 48.5 secs and 1 min 49.5 secs, which I'd be pleased with.'

This answer is sophisticated because it identifies a clear strategy for the whole race as well as appropriate thought content and foci for attention. Only if the coach thought the goals were unrealistic would he intervene. Therefore, the response might be:

'I agree with your basic goals and think that providing nothing untoward happens you should be able to achieve them. So let's now look on the brighter side of your current form and think about what you could achieve if you have a really good race.'

The athlete is now invited to raise his sights a little and think more positively about his form and racing plan. He might reply as follows:

'Well, in so far as I have no intention of allowing a slow, tactical race to develop, I can only answer in terms of overall time. If I can concentrate on staying relaxed and maintaining good form throughout the race then, given my plan for the first 600m I could finish in under 1 min 48 secs.'

The coach replies:

'Yes, that sounds realistic enough, and you're certainly capable of doing that if you can concentrate fully and conditions are favourable on the day. So let's be even more optimistic now and think of what you just might achieve if you have one of those races we've all dreamed of but seldom experienced.'

The athlete might not even want to respond to this invitation which would be perfectly reasonable. However, it does no harm to make it providing it comes after the other two. Alternatively, he might reply 'under 1 min 47.5 secs' and leave it at that because there is little else he could improve upon as far as his goals for the race are concerned. The important point to note for present purposes, however, is that at no time did he mention winning the race. All the goals he identified are under his control and are therefore classed as performance goals. The other important point to note is that the athlete identified more than one goal for the race, particularly in terms of what should happen. In summary, they were as follows:

1.   To go off fast from the gun with the prospect of leading at the break from lanes in mind.
2.   To run 54 seconds for the first 400m.
3.   To maintain the same running speed for the third 200m of the race and thereby achieve 1 min 21 secs for 600m.
4.   To concentrate on staying relaxed and maintaining good form throughout the race and particularly so in the final 200m.
5.   To achieve an overall time of between 1 min 48.5 secs and 1 min 49.5 secs.

To summarize, the goals for competitions should be:

1.   Agreed upon jointly by the coach and athlete concerned.
2.   Restricted to factors over which the athlete has personal control.
3.   Stated positively rather than in either negative or avoidance terms.
4.   Related to segments of performance.
5.   Ranked in order of priority where there is more than one goal.
6.   Aimed at improving performance, not simply maintaining it.
7.   As difficult as possible but still attainable (hence the reason for setting goals at three levels).
8.   Related directly to performance.
9.   Observable and readily assessible.

Further information on goal-setting and how it can be used as a mental preparation strategy is presented in Chapter 6.

Evaluation

A neglected feature of coaching in general is thorough analysis and evaluation of performance after a competition. Setting goals at different levels enables both coach and athlete to analyse and evaluate in detail. In the example given above they would have five basic goals to evaluate, analysing the reasons for achieving them or not. A plan for recording such evaluation might be useful because writing things down on paper always raises commitment to what is written. An example of such a plan

	GOALS			LEVEL ACHIEVED			ASSESSMENT AND EVALUATION OF PERFORMANCE GOALS	FUTURE ACTION
	Should be achieved	Could be achieved	Just might be achieved	Should	Could	Just might be		
1.								
2.								
3.								
4.								
5.								

Fig 6   A plan for recording goals set and their evaluation.

is illustrated in **Figure 6**. This example is given as an idea for coaches and others to adapt to suit their own purposes, and not as something to be copied without question. In using a plan of this kind it goes without saying that not every part of it need be filled in; for many competitions this would be unnecessary and even inappropriate. The important thing is that it allows a record of the pre-competition and post-competition discussion to be kept for future reference. This may well contribute a great deal to keeping the athlete highly motivated. Incidentally, never conduct an evaluation straight after a competition. Wait at least two hours, but preferably until the morning after.

Conclusion

In concluding this chapter, it should be stressed that this short account of what motivates people amounts to little more than an introduction to what is an extremely complex subject. The precise nature and strength of any individual's level of motivation for a particular task at any one moment can be likened to a fingerprint – it is like no other. Unlike a fingerprint, however, it can change suddenly and dramatically in accordance with changes in the individual's physical and psychological environment, and leave everyone concerned wondering what has happened. Nevertheless, this is not a philosophy of despair. Motivation of one kind or another is responsible for all behaviour above the level of reflex, and so by becoming more aware of the forces that shape our lives and how they do so and by getting to know the people we interact with on a regular basis really well, we can increase the chances of helping them sustain their levels of motivation and even, perhaps, to raise them.

CHAPTER THREE

Stress and Anxiety

Dr Graham Jones

The following excerpt is from *The Times,* and appeared on the morning of the ladies' singles final at Wimbledon in 1988:

Steffi Graf and Martina Navratilova are so evenly matched, in terms of racket skills and athleticism, that the Wimbledon women's singles final will probably be decided by their emotional response to the occasion. On the basis that Navratilova has more at stake and is occasionally prone to nervous inhibitions, I take Graf to win.

This provides a convenient example of the notion that, at the top level in sport, there is very little difference in the skill levels of the participants and that the major factor likely to distinguish the winner from the loser is the ability to cope with psychological pressure. Take golf, for example, in which all of the players in the top twenty, say, are very much on a 'par' as far as skill level is concerned. In theory, if skill level is the only factor influencing performance, they should all shoot the same score on each and every round. But they do not. Why does one golfer shoot a three-under-par whilst another, that same day, shoots three-over-par, with the intriguing possibility that this situation might be reversed the following day?

Whilst physical conditions, such as the weather and speed of the greens, might be more suited to one golfer than another on a particular day, it is much more likely that the discrepancy in the two scores is again due to psychological factors. These factors might include motivation, effort, concentration, confidence and so on, but one consistent and crucial factor is the ability to handle the stress of competition. Today's top-level sport is not only highly competitive, but invariably well covered by the media, and the rewards for success (and, conversely, the disappointments associated with failure) are often great. These are clearly factors which are likely to cause stress. In fact one study carried out in America found that elite wrestlers between the ages of 15 and 19 were anxious or worried in 66 per cent of their matches.

Many sports' performers seem to cope very well under the pressure of competition. The world's top javelin thrower Steve

Backley has said that he needs to feel under pressure to perform well, adding that competition improved his performance by at least 10 per cent against training. On the other hand, there are also some performers who have a tendency to fold – or at least under-achieve – when under pressure and who consequently do not realize their full potential. The sporting world is littered with performers who have enormous potential and perform brilliantly in training but who seldom reproduce this level of performance in competition. The vast majority of individual sports' performers who have approached me for help and advice have experienced problems coping with the pressure of competition and have identified themselves as being too anxious, both before and during performance. These performers have been from a range of sports including swimming, golf, rugby, ice skating, squash, judo and cricket. Most of them have possessed the physical attributes and skills required to compete at the top level, but have needed to acquire appropriate mental skills in order to realize their full potential. Clearly, stress is a crucial factor in sport.

The remainder of this chapter will address a number of issues concerning stress and anxiety in sport, including what are stress and anxiety?; can we predict which sports' performers are likely to become highly anxious when competing?; what happens to performers when they become anxious?; what causes anxiety in sports performers?; and, finally, what can be done to control anxiety in sports performers? I will refer throughout the chapter to a series of interviews carried out by myself and a colleague Dr Lew Hardy, with six past and present elite sports' performers which examined their experiences of stress in sport and the psychological strategies they used to cope with it. The performers were Steve Backley, the world's current number one javelin thrower and the 1990 Commonwealth Games gold medal winner and Commonwealth record holder; Sue Challis, the 1983 European and 1984 World champion in ladies trampolining; Alan Edge, a member of the Great Britain 1979 World Championship canoe slalom winning team; David Hemery, Olympic Games 400m hurdles gold medal winner and world record holder in 1968; James May, gold medal winner in the men's individual apparatus vault final at the 1990 Commonwealth Games; and Mary Nevill, captain of Great Britain's ladies hockey team and member of the England side which finished fourth in the 1990 World Cup. Each of these athletes has given permission to discuss the content of the interviews.

An individual's response to the stress of competition will vary acording to the specific situation.

Defining Stress and Anxiety

One of the problems which has plagued research in this area has been a lack of consensus over the meaning of stress. Consequently, the definition proposed below is my own, but it essentially falls into line with the 'interactionist' approach which currently represents the most popular and accepted approach to stress in sport psychology. The interactionist position states that an individual's emotional response, or 'affective experience' as it is referred to in **Figure 7**, is the result of an interaction between the individual and the environment. Stress is therefore a stimulus which is present in the form of demands placed upon the individual by the environment. A crucial component in the equation is the individual's thought processes or cognitive appraisal of the stressor which forms a mediator between the stimulus and the response.

Competition, for example, is one such stressor. Whether the competitive environment causes an anxiety response depends upon sports performers' appraisal of their ability to meet the demands of the situation. Because this appraisal is so important, it should be clear that what causes anxiety in one performer may not in another. What was very evident from the interviews was that stress was not necessarily perceived as a negative phenomenon: on the contrary, several of the athletes reported that stress could be a very positive factor. In fact, they all stated that they tried to perceive or appraise the stress of competition in a positive way. So, according to the model depicted in **Figure 7**, the stress of competition can be perceived in two different ways – negatively, leading to anxiety symptoms, or positively, in which case the performer is coping with the stress. The situation is made more complex because the same individual's response to the stress of competition will vary according to the specific situation. For example, a tennis player's appraisal of a match against an opponent who, on their previous meeting, was beaten in straight sets, is likely to be positive and thus induce less anxiety than had the result gone the other way.

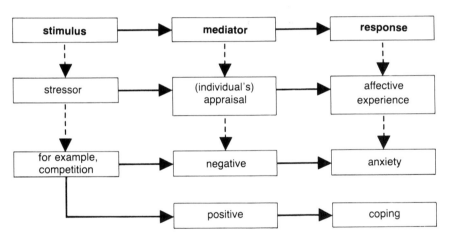

Fig 7   Interactionist approach to stress.

Competitive Anxiety as a Personality Dimension

A considerable amount of research in sport psychology has been devoted to the notion that competitive anxiety can be considered as a dimension of an individual's personality. In other words, it is possible to predict which performers will experience high and low levels of anxiety in competitive situations. Before you read any further, please respond to the questionnaire in Exercise 6.

The questionnaire is a modified version of the Sport Competition Anxiety Test which was developed by the American sport psychologist Rainer Martens in 1977, and measures competitive

Exercise 6

Below are some statements about how people feel when they compete in sport. Read each statement and decide if you feel this way 'hardly ever' (A), 'sometimes' (B), or 'often' (C). Circle the appropriate answer. Then, for each statement, except 6 and 11, if you stated that you feel this way 'often' (C) state the degree to which you regard it as being either 'facilitative' or 'debilitative' to your performance. If you stated that you feel this way 'hardly ever' (A) or 'sometimes' (B), please state how you would feel if you felt this way often. For statements 6 and 11, if you answered 'hardly ever' (A) state the degree to which you regard it as being either 'facilitative' or 'debilitative' to your performance. If you answered 'sometimes' (B) or 'often' (C), please state how you would feel if you felt like this 'hardly ever'. There are no right and wrong answers. Do not spend too much time on any one statement.

	Hardly Ever	Some-times	Often	Very Debili-tative						Very Facili-tative
1. Competing against others is socially enjoyable.	A	B	C	1 2 3 4 5 6 7
2. Before I compete I feel nervous.	A	B	C	1 2 3 4 5 6 7
3. Before I compete I worry about not performing well.	A	B	C	1 2 3 4 5 6 7
4. I am a good sport when I compete.	A	B	C	1 2 3 4 5 6 7
5. When I compete I worry about making mistakes.	A	B	C	1 2 3 4 5 6 7
6. Before I compete I am calm.	A	B	C	1 2 3 4 5 6 7
7. Setting a goal is important when competing.	A	B	C	1 2 3 4 5 6 7
8. Before I compete I get a queasy feeling in my stomach.	A	B	C	1 2 3 4 5 6 7
9. Just before competing I notice my heart beats faster than usual.	A	B	C	1 2 3 4 5 6 7
10. I like to compete in games that demand considerable physical energy.	A	B	C	1 2 3 4 5 6 7
11. Before I compete I feel relaxed.	A	B	C	1 2 3 4 5 6 7
12. Before I compete I am nervous.	A	B	C	1 2 3 4 5 6 7
13. Team sports are more exciting than individual sports.	A	B	C	1 2 3 4 5 6 7
14. I get nervous waiting to start the contest.	A	B	C	1 2 3 4 5 6 7
15. Before I compete I usually get uptight.	A	B	C	1 2 3 4 5 6 7

trait anxiety. The first response scale (A, B, C) indicates the frequency with which you generally experience the symptoms referred to before you compete. Your responses on this scale should be scored in the following manner.

Ignore your responses to items numbered 1, 4, 7, 10 and 13. These items do not measure anxiety symptoms. For items numbered 2, 3, 5, 8, 9, 12, 14 and 15: A=1; B=2; C=3. For items numbered 6 and 11: A=3; B=2; C=1. Now add up your score, which should fall between 10 and 30. The higher your score the more prone you are to experience anxiety before competing.

Next, consider the other dimension in the questionnaire, which I shall refer to as the 'facilitation' dimension. This scale should be scored in the following manner: Ignore your responses to items numbered 1, 4, 7, 10 and 13. For the remainder of the items simply add up your responses based on the numbers you circled. Your score on this scale should fall between 10 and 70. I have added the facilitation dimension with the intended purpose of demonstrating that experiencing what are described as 'anxiety' symptoms is not always detrimental.

For example, if you scored high on the frequency dimension, perhaps above 24, but also high, above 55, on the facilitation dimension, then the anxiety symptoms that you generally experience before competition are facilitative and certainly not detrimental. As indicated in **Figure 8** there is a gulf between your feelings before competition and how you would like to feel. You might label these symptoms as constituting excitement (positive) rather than anxiety (negative). If, on the other hand, you scored high on the frequency dimension but low, under 25, on facilitation, your symptoms are unwanted and you perceive them as debilitative. In this case there is a mismatch and you would probably benefit from learning some form of anxiety reduction technique. If your score on the frequency dimension was low, under 16, and you scored low on the facilitation dimension, there is a match between your feelings and how you would like to feel. What you are actually saying is that you do not experience anxiety symptoms often, but if you did you would perceive them as debilitative. And finally, if you scored low on frequency but high on facilitation there is a mismatch because you are intimating you perceive anxiety symptoms as facilitative if experienced often. In this case, you might benefit from some 'psyching-up' strategy before competing.

Many readers will not have fallen into any of these four categories, in which case you scored at a moderate level on frequency and/or facilitation. A moderate level of anxiety may be appropriate for you but, if not, any mismatch will not be as great as those two depicted in **Figure 8**.

Frequency	Facilitative	Match?	Intervention
high	high	yes	
high	low	no	anxiety reduction
low	low	yes	
low	high	no	psyching-up

Fig 8   Matching the frequency and facilitation of anxiety symptoms.

The implications of this rather complex situation for the coach and sport psychologist are potentially enormous. Clearly, athletes respond differently before competition – some experience high or low levels of anxiety, whilst others experience a mismatch between how they actually feel and how they want to feel. The skill of the coach and sport psychologist is in knowing or being able to identify in the crucial moments before and during competition which performers may need motivating, which are too anxious, and which are feeling just right and can be left alone.

The following section on competitive state anxiety will examine factors which may help coaches and sport psychologists make such decisions.

Competitive State Anxiety

It is very unlikely that athletes will experience anxiety symptoms at the same level of intensity before every competition. These will vary as a function of a number of factors which might include the importance of the competition, perceived ability of the opposition, performance in your previous competition, weather conditions, and so on. In this section we will examine competitive state anxiety, or the anxiety you experience at a specific point in time rather than generally. We will be especially interested in the specific symptoms you experience and what happens to them during the pre-competition and performance periods.

First, I would like you to respond to the questionnaire in

Exercise 7 but, this time, within a very specific context. Think back to the most important match or competition in which you have played. Complete the questionnaire according to how you were feeling *one week* before the match or competition.

Now, respond to the questionnaire again in Exercise 8, but this time in a slightly different context. Can you remember how you were feeling *five minutes* before the competition? Complete the questionnaire accordingly.

There are two response dimensions on this questionnaire; the intensity and the facilitation of the symptoms. Score your responses on both questionnaires in the following manner. Add up your responses on the intensity and facilitation dimensions for items numbered 1, 4, 7, 10, 13, 16, 19, 22 and 25. These items measure cognitive anxiety or worry. Write your scores in **Figure 9** below for intensity and facilitation at one week and at five minutes before competition.

Next, add up your responses on the intensity and facilitation dimensions for items numbered 2, 5, 8, 11, 17, 20, 23 and 26. Also, include item 14 but reverse the scoring so that 1=4, 2=3, 3=2, and 4=1. These items measure somatic anxiety or physiological arousal. Write your scores in the table for intensity and facilitation at one week and at five minutes before competition. Then, add up your responses on the intensity and facilitation dimensions for items numbered 3, 6, 9, 12, 15, 18, 21, 24 and 27. These items measure self-confidence.

Your scores on the intensity and facilitation dimensions for each of the three scales should fall between 9 and 36 and 9 and 63 respectively.

	ONE WEEK BEFORE		FIVE MINUTES BEFORE	
	INTENSITY	DIRECTION	INTENSITY	DIRECTION
COGNITIVE ANXIETY				
SOMATIC ANXIETY				
SELF-CONFIDENCE				

Fig 9   Assessing state of anxiety prior to competition.

The questionnaire is a modified version of the Competitive State Anxiety Inventory-2, which was published by Rainer Martens

Exercise 7

Directions: A number of statements which athletes have used to describe their feelings before competition are given below. The Questionnaire is divided into 2 sections. Read each statement and then circle the appropriate number on the scale from 1 to 4 to indicate how you felt one week before the competition. Then, for each statement, circle an appropriate number on the scale from 1 to 7 to signify how facilitative or debilitative you perceive your response to be. There are no right or wrong answers. Do not spend too much time on any one statement.

	Not at all	Some- what	Moder- ately so	Very much so	Very Debili- tative					Very Facili- tative	
1. I am concerned about this competition.	1	2	3	4	1 2 3 4 5 6 7						
2. I feel nervous.	1	2	3	4	1 2 3 4 5 6 7						
3. I feel at ease.	1	2	3	4	1 2 3 4 5 6 7						
4. I have self-doubts.	1	2	3	4	1 2 3 4 5 6 7						
5. I feel jittery.	1	2	3	4	1 2 3 4 5 6 7						
6. I feel comfortable.	1	2	3	4	1 2 3 4 5 6 7						
7. I am concerned that I may not do as well in this competition as I could.	1	2	3	4	1 2 3 4 5 6 7						
8. My body feels tense.	1	2	3	4	1 2 3 4 5 6 7						
9. I feel self-confident.	1	2	3	4	1 2 3 4 5 6 7						
10. I am concerned about losing.	1	2	3	4	1 2 3 4 5 6 7						
11. I feel tense in my stomach.	1	2	3	4	1 2 3 4 5 6 7						
12. I feel secure.	1	2	3	4	1 2 3 4 5 6 7						
13. I am concerned about choking under pressure.	1	2	3	4	1 2 3 4 5 6 7						
14. My body feels relaxed.	1	2	3	4	1 2 3 4 5 6 7						
15. I'm confident I can meet the challenge.	1	2	3	4	1 2 3 4 5 6 7						
16. I'm concerned about performing poorly.	1	2	3	4	1 2 3 4 5 6 7						
17. My heart is racing.	1	2	3	4	1 2 3 4 5 6 7						
18. I'm confident about performing well.	1	2	3	4	1 2 3 4 5 6 7						
19. I'm worried about reaching my goal.	1	2	3	4	1 2 3 4 5 6 7						
20. I feel my stomach sinking.	1	2	3	4	1 2 3 4 5 6 7						
21. I feel mentally relaxed.	1	2	3	4	1 2 3 4 5 6 7						
22. I'm concerned that others will be disappointed with my performance.	1	2	3	4	1 2 3 4 5 6 7						
23. My hands are clammy.	1	2	3	4	1 2 3 4 5 6 7						
24. I feel confident because I mentally picture myself reaching my goal.	1	2	3	4	1 2 3 4 5 6 7						
25. I'm concerned I won't be able to concentrate.	1	2	3	4	1 2 3 4 5 6 7						
26. My body feels tight.	1	2	3	4	1 2 3 4 5 6 7						
27. I'm confident of coming through under pressure.	1	2	3	4	1 2 3 4 5 6 7						

Exercise 8

Use this exercise as for Exercise 7, but respond according to how you felt five minutes before competition.

	Not at all	Some- what	Moder- ately so	Very much so	Very Debili- tative						Very Facili- tative
1. I am concerned about this competition.	1	2	3	4	1	2	3	4	5	6	7
2. I feel nervous.	1	2	3	4	1	2	3	4	5	6	7
3. I feel at ease.	1	2	3	4	1	2	3	4	5	6	7
4. I have self-doubts.	1	2	3	4	1	2	3	4	5	6	7
5. I feel jittery.	1	2	3	4	1	2	3	4	5	6	7
6. I feel comfortable.	1	2	3	4	1	2	3	4	5	6	7
7. I am concerned that I may not do as well in this competition as I could.	1	2	3	4	1	2	3	4	5	6	7
8. My body feels tense.	1	2	3	4	1	2	3	4	5	6	7
9. I feel self-confident.	1	2	3	4	1	2	3	4	5	6	7
10. I am concerned about losing.	1	2	3	4	1	2	3	4	5	6	7
11. I feel tense in my stomach.	1	2	3	4	1	2	3	4	5	6	7
12. I feel secure.	1	2	3	4	1	2	3	4	5	6	7
13. I am concerned about choking under pressure.	1	2	3	4	1	2	3	4	5	6	7
14. My body feels relaxed.	1	2	3	4	1	2	3	4	5	6	7
15. I'm confident I can meet the challenge.	1	2	3	4	1	2	3	4	5	6	7
16. I'm concerned about performing poorly.	1	2	3	4	1	2	3	4	5	6	7
17. My heart is racing.	1	2	3	4	1	2	3	4	5	6	7
18. I'm confident about performing well.	1	2	3	4	1	2	3	4	5	6	7
19. I'm worried about reaching my goal.	1	2	3	4	1	2	3	4	5	6	7
20. I feel my stomach sinking.	1	2	3	4	1	2	3	4	5	6	7
21. I feel mentally relaxed.	1	2	3	4	1	2	3	4	5	6	7
22. I'm concerned that others will be disappointed with my performance.	1	2	3	4	1	2	3	4	5	6	7
23. My hands are clammy.	1	2	3	4	1	2	3	4	5	6	7
24. I feel confident because I mentally picture myself reaching my goal.	1	2	3	4	1	2	3	4	5	6	7
25. I'm concerned I won't be able to concentrate.	1	2	3	4	1	2	3	4	5	6	7
26. My body feels tight.	1	2	3	4	1	2	3	4	5	6	7
27. I'm confident of coming through under pressure.	1	2	3	4	1	2	3	4	5	6	7

and his colleagues. With a colleague, I have added the facilitation dimension and we have used this modified form in our research. It essentially measures two different types of competitive anxiety symptom and a third component, self-confidence, which relates very closely to anxiety.

Cognitive anxiety, or worry, is generally viewed as being characterized by negative expectations, lack of concentration and images of failure. Somatic anxiety is essentially the performer's perception of physiological arousal and includes symptoms of nervousness and tension, not least 'butterflies' in the stomach. The separation of anxiety into cognitive and somatic symptoms is important in the context of the implementation of anxiety control techniques, as we shall later see.

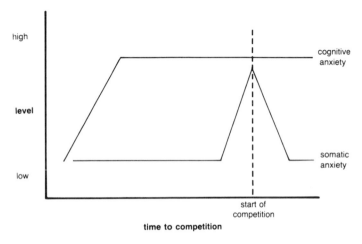

Fig 10   Changes in cognitive and somatic anxiety during the period preceding and during competition.

Research has been carried out to examine how these two anxiety components change during the period preceding and during competition; **Figure 10** depicts a simplified view of the general findings. Cognitive anxiety generally becomes elevated much earlier before the competition than somatic anxiety. Once elevated, cognitive anxiety remains relatively stable up until, and during, competition. However, the intensity of the symptoms will obviously fluctuate if the performer's expectations of success are altered. For example, a middle distance runner who sustains an ankle injury a week before a major race would almost certainly report a rise in cognitive anxiety and then probably a reduction once a fitness assurance had been given by a doctor. The other component of anxiety, somatic anxiety, does not generally increase until much nearer the time of competition, possibly the night before, or maybe not until the day of the competition. Certainly, most sports performers will experience a rise in their physiological symptoms in the dressing room just before the event or match begins. Examine your own intensity scores on cognitive and somatic anxiety at the two stages prior to the event in question. Do your scores reflect the predictions portrayed in **Figure 10**?

Interestingly, the patterning of anxiety symptoms over time has been investigated as a means of distinguishing between successful and less successful performers. One study with parachute jumpers on the day of a jump showed different patterning of anxiety in experienced and inexperienced jumpers as the jump neared. In the inexperienced parachutists, anxiety increased progressively during the day and was at its greatest just before the jump. The experienced parachutists, on the other hand, reported their greatest anxiety when they entered the plane at the airport, after which it decreased. In a study on gymnasts, the successful athletes reported being more anxious than the less successful ones prior to the competition, but this situation was reversed during performance. Interestingly, the findings also suggested that the successful gymnasts tended to use their anxiety as a stimulant to better performance whilst the less successful seemed to arouse themselves into states of near panic.

Conclusions

Two important points emerge from these findings. Firstly, it appears that elite performers experience the same intensity of anxiety as lesser performers, but are able to control their anxiety at crucial moments. Second, as evidenced by the case of the gymnasts, how the anxiety symptoms are perceived is crucial. Consequently, it is important to emphasize again that high scores on the intensity dimension of the cognitive and/or somatic anxiety scales do not mean that this state is detrimental. Consequently, these scores can only be viewed in conjunction with the scores on the facilitation dimension. Examine your scores on the facilitation dimension of the questionnaire. If your scores are high, say over 50, then the intensity of anxiety you experienced at the time, whether high, moderate or low, was appropriate for you. If your score was low, say under 25, then there was a mismatch.

I once helped a swimmer who experienced very intense somatic anxiety symptoms on the day of competition. She was nervous and tense to the point of being sick on many occasions.

Her response to this was negative, in that she came to hate the thought of competition. Conversely, I am familiar with the case of an ex-international footballer who was regularly sick before big games. However, he regarded this as his normal response and perceived it as being facilitative. In fact, if he came to a big match and he was not physically sick beforehand then he was worried that he was not sufficiently psychologically prepared.

What about the third component measured in the questionnaire, self-confidence? One thing has become very evident to me in my association with world-class performers over the last couple of years – they are all supremely confident in their own ability. It was particularly evident in the interviews that there was absolutely no room for even the slightest doubts if the athletes were to attain the levels of performance which they sought.

You may well find when examining your own scores on self-confidence for the two occasions that they inversely mirror your cognitive anxiety responses. This is because they are conceptualized to lie at opposite ends of the same continuum, with high cognitive anxiety being associated with low self-confidence and vice-versa. Another key factor is how you perceived your level of self-confidence. You would presumably have perceived a low level of self-confidence as being debilitative, but you might also have perceived a high level as being debilitative if it represented over-confidence or perhaps complacency.

This again represents a very complex situation in which individuals will respond very differently to the stress of competition. Not only will individual athletes respond with different levels of competitive anxiety, they will also experience different symptoms of anxiety. The skill of the coach or sport psychologist is in being able to identify which performers require some form of intervention strategy.

Competitive Anxiety and Sports Performance

A considerable amount of research has been carried out to examine the relationship between competitive anxiety and sports performance. This research has generally failed to unravel the precise details of the relationship, but it has demonstrated that it is complex. Findings have generally supported the intuitive notion that anxiety impairs performance. However, a couple of recent studies have shown that anxiety does not necessarily impair performance and can actually enhance it. The situation is largely dependent, as we have seen in the previous sections, on the individual and how the athlete perceives the anxiety symptoms in terms of the debilitative–facilitative continuum. But a further important factor to consider is the nature of the performance itself.

During his interview, James May stated that the increased physiological arousal associated with elevated anxiety interfered with the fine movement control required on the pommel horse, but enhanced the more explosive type of performance required on the vault. Sue Challis reported that anxiety could negatively affect her timing whilst performing on the trampoline, but also have a positive effect in that it made her feel stronger. In fact, the general consensus amongst the athletes interviewed was that controlled cognitive anxiety enhanced performance on well-learned tasks, and that increased somatic anxiety or physiological arousal enhanced performance on skills requiring speed and strength, but it was detrimental to skills requiring fine movements and timing. Extra research backs up these findings.

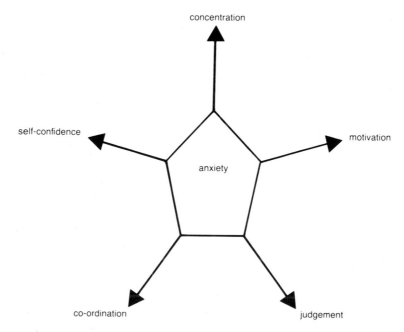

Fig 11   Possible influences of competitive anxiety.

The fact remains, however, that in many cases anxiety will impair performance; but how and why? Precise answers to these questions are not yet available but several factors have been identified as being important (*see* **Figure 11**), including self-confidence, concentration, motivation, effort, judgement and co-ordination.

Self-confidence has already been identified as being closely linked with competitive anxiety. Basically, a high level of cognitive anxiety is associated with a low level of self-confidence in competition. Anecdotal reports strongly suggest that low self-confidence will result in sub-optimal performance. Anxiety can adversely affect the performer's perception of, or confidence in, the ability to perform complex skills so that an athlete may opt to perform a simpler, less risky skill. Sue Challis, for example, stated that she had occasionally doubted her ability to perform moves of a sufficient quality to the extent that she had set off to do one move and then done another, simpler move. Mary Nevill similarly told me that she occasionally doubted her ability to perform certain hockey skills in high-pressure situations.

Concentration or attention is a limited resource in that we only have so much of it available. Consequently, if a sports performer devotes a large part of that limited attention to worrying or being cognitively anxious about a particular opponent, playing conditions, etc., then the athlete has only a little attention remaining to focus upon actual performance. A major problem confronting an ice skater I worked with was that, both before and during competition, he focused his attention on worrying about how good was the opposition rather than concentrating on his own performance. So, quite simply, anxiety can impair performance by distracting the athlete.

Motivation can be affected by anxiety in two different ways, both potentially leading to impaired performance. First, anxiety can increase motivation to the extent that the performer tries too hard. It might be surprising to learn that athletes can exert too much effort but it is consistent with many elite performers' reports that their best performances have seemed almost effortless. Anxiety can also reduce motivation so that the performer does not devote sufficient effort to performance. In the case of the anxious swimmer referred to earlier, when on the starting blocks waiting for the gun to go off she was busy trying to deny the importance of the situation and of winning. She used verbal persuasion techniques such as 'it's only a race; it doesn't matter which position I finish in.' This was essentially a defence mechanism, but it had the effect of reducing her motivation to perform well and consequently the effort she exerted once the race began. During this phase, her times in competition were consistently slower than in training.

Judgement is a crucial part of sports performance, but it can be impaired by anxiety. How often have you seen players under pressure do something uncharacteristic, such as make inappropriate decisions and unforced errors? The increased cognitive anxiety associated with competition may lead to confusion and affects performers' perceptions of situations and, consequently, their decisions. Also, when anxious, some performers occasionally forget about carefully pre-arranged plans and strategies and revert to previous, perhaps unsuccessful tactics.

Co-ordination can be negatively affected by the increased physiological arousal associated with somatic anxiety. This often results in increased muscle tension which is likely to be detrimental to fine touch or fine movement control, as is required in bowls or archery, for example. Research has found that manual dexterity, in particular, is impaired under increased anxiety, which would help to explain why some goalkeepers or rugby players often fumble or drop the ball under pressure.

Maintaining Psychological Control Under Competitive Stress

It was evident from the interviews with the top performers that they were experts at maintaining psychological control under the intense pressure of top level competition. Several strategies may be used to achieve such control under stress, and they are discussed briefly.

Anxiety Control

Research has shown that one of the important factors which distinguishes elite sports performers from the rest is their ability to control their anxiety at crucial moments during competition. One means of achieving an appropriate level of anxiety, particularly for those individuals who experience a high level of anxiety which is debilitative, is through relaxation. It is important to emphasize that, in the context of competitive sport, relaxation is not synonymous with total relaxation. It would be inappropriate, for example, for a rugby player to be totally relaxed five minutes before a game. Rugby requires, amongst many other things, intense physical exertion and also rapid decision-making which will not be performed optimally when in a totally relaxed state. Relaxation in sport is therefore concerned with lowering anxiety to an appropriate level which will differ from individual to individual.

As well as using relaxation before competition, it can also be beneficial if practised during performance. In such instances athletes must be able to relax within a very short period of time, perhaps a couple of seconds at the most. This obviously requires frequent and dedicated practice, but it has proved very effective with a number of performers with whom I have worked. In one case an ice skater felt himself becoming 'uptight' as he approached a complex jump, usually impairing his performance. The relaxation technique we worked on was meditation-based which initially meant he could relax within a 15-minute period. Over several months he was gradually able to reduce this time to a mere few seconds. He was then able to use his relaxation technique immediately prior to the jump which meant he was in control and improved his performance.

RELAXATION

Relaxation can be divided into two general types, mental relaxation and physical. Mental relaxation techniques are often referred to as mind-to-body techniques because they are primarily aimed at relaxation through the mind. Meditation is an example of mental relaxation and is beneficial because it also aids concentration.

The method requires a quiet environment and a comfortable position in the learning phase, but as the performer becomes more proficient it is important that practice takes place in various types of situation. For example, I often require performers to practise in uncomfortable positions or when physically fatigued in an attempt to simulate some of the conditions experienced in competition. Meditation also involves a passive attitude and a mental device such as a verbal cue (e.g. 'relax' or 'calm') which the individual repeats silently on each exhalation. This helps to reduce any anxiety because the individual focuses attention on the verbal cue and on slow, rhythmical breathing rather than on any anxiety symptoms. When skilled at meditation-based relaxation, the sports performer should be able to relax to an appropriate level following two or three deep breaths and repetitions of the verbal cue.

Physical relaxation techniques are often referred to as body-to-mind techniques because they focus primarily on relaxation through the body. Probably, the most common technique of this kind is progressive muscular relaxation. This basically involves tensing and relaxing specific muscle groups, progressing from one to the other. Again, when skilled at progressive muscular relaxation the performer can relax a specific muscle group very quickly during competition. This can be very beneficial in sports requiring fine control and in which excessive muscle tension is usually undesirable.

It is important to emphasize that not every relaxation technique is suitable and effective for every individual. For example, meditation may be appropriate for one individual but not for another, and vice-versa in the case of progressive muscular relaxation. A general guideline for the adoption and implementation of relaxation techniques is based on what is generally known as the 'matching hypothesis'. This states, as shown in **Figure 12**, that the relaxation techniques should be matched to the anxiety symptoms experienced. In other words a mental relaxation technique should be used for performers experiencing predominantly cognitive anxiety symptoms, and a physical relaxation technique should be used for performers experiencing predominantly somatic anxiety symptoms.

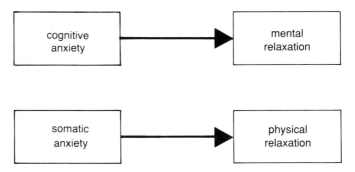

Fig 12   Matching the relaxation technique to the anxiety symptom.

Finally, it is also important to emphasize that relaxation skills often take a considerable time to master to reach the level at which they are appropriate for use during performance. Also, once learned, relaxation must be practised regularly since, like any physical skill, lack of practice results in 'rustiness'. A professional golfer I recently worked with who was experiencing debilitative anxiety problems expected an overnight cure and an almost immediate improvement in performance. Unfortunately, mental training, and particularly relaxation training, does not usually have such dramatic results. Thus, one of the first tasks of the sport psychologist is to remind the performer that mental skills are like physical skills; they require regular, committed and dedicated practice sometimes over a long period of time, although the exact length required to master relaxation skills will vary greatly between individuals.

Relaxation procedures also tend to be unnecessarily surrounded by a degree of mysticism and almost suspicion by people who know nothing about these skills. Consequently, relaxation techniques also require some degree of belief on the part of the performer that they will eventually derive some benefit.

All of the athletes interviewed used some form of relaxation technique, although they had experienced little, if any, formal training in the skill. Their use of relaxation seemed to be part of their own natural preparation and often seemed to take place in a fairly unstructured manner. Nevertheless, relaxation was a very important component of their strategies for maintaining control both before and during competition.

Simulation of Competition Stressors

The competitive environment contains many stressors, including the presence of a crowd, judges, etc., which are not present in the training environment. In many instances, performers practise for long hours in a comfortable, friendly training environment and are only exposed to the stressors associated with competition during the competition itself. Not being accustomed to the competitive stress environment can easily create anxiety. One method of tackling this problem involves simulating that environment. Simulation training is a means of desensitizing performers to competitive stress and also of enhancing their confidence and improving their concentration skills during competition. This may be achieved via two means.

The first method is through *visualization*, enabling the performer to rehearse mentally coping with the stressful competitive environment. The athlete David Hemery, for example, reported continually rehearsing his very detailed race plan in the face of various different possible situations. So, for example, he mentally rehearsed '. . . running in every lane and condition that I could conceivably think of . . . but always maintaining my control.' Steve Backley also said that he used visualization to simulate the stress of competition, say in the last round of a major competition, in a losing position and with only one throw left.

As well as using visualization-based simulation training, the athletes also reported using *physical practice* in the presence of simulated competition stressors. Sue Challis, Steve Backley and James May, in particular, viewed this as a particularly important part of their training. Interestingly, a professional basketball team in America regularly hired a rowdy crowd to watch them train. In this way they became accustomed to playing in front of a large, hostile crowd so that stress in actual competition was minimized.

The Competition Plan

Several of the athletes stated that they developed very detailed and structured competition plans, and also had explicit alternative plans which they could use to enable them to cope with any conceivable situation that might arise. The idea of a competition plan is, of course, based on goal setting.

As outlined in the previous chapter, goal setting is acknowledged as an important technique for the enhancement of both motivation and self-confidence. It can also be used as a means of maintaining control during competition. One of the crucial principles underlying effective goal setting is that the goals should be difficult but realistic. By carefully structuring realistic competition plans, plus alternatives, the performer is in effect reducing any uncertainty, and the associated stress about performance expectations. One of the athletes interviewed, Alan Edge, particularly emphasized the importance of the competition plan in enhancing his confidence on the day of a competition. The athletes generally perceived this confidence as some sort of inoculation against anxiety effects.

Concentration

As stated earlier, cognitive anxiety can debilitate performance because it distracts performers from focusing attention on the important aspects of performance. Consequently, developing concentration skills would help performers to impose greater control over what they are attending to. It is beyond the scope of this chapter to discuss specific methods of enhancing concentration, but strategies already discussed in the form of relaxation, simulation training and the competition plan all help to develop concentration skills. A fuller explanation of these, and other mental preparation strategies is provided in Chapter 6.

Conclusions

This chapter has presented a very brief discussion of stress and anxiety in sport. Stress is clearly a very important factor in contemporary competitive sport and is an area which has attracted and intrigued researchers in sport psychology for a number of years. It is evident from this research that stress and anxiety, and their relationships with sports performance, is a complex area. Crucial factors considered in this chapter which contribute to this complexity were, first, that individual sports performers react differently to the stress of competition, and, second, that different types of performance may be affected in different ways.

Available research findings, together with the interviews discussed, suggest that elite performers are experts at maintaining control under the intense pressure of top-level competition. The implications for the coach and sport psychologist are that, in terms of psychological preparation for competition, performers must be treated as individuals. For example, general 'psyching-up' routines which are used frequently in the pre-competition period in many team sports may be appropriate for some of the members of the team, but totally inappropriate for others who may require anxiety reduction, or those already in the right state of mind. The skill of the coach and sport psychologist is in determining which psychological strategy is appropriate for which individual.

CHAPTER FOUR

Aggression

Dr Larry Leith

Few themes in sport have received as much attention as that of aggression and violence. To view it we can attend a boxing match, watch runners jostle and elbow for position in a distance race, or merely wait for fights to break out in rugby, ice hockey, basketball and soccer. We can also witness aggression via the media. But why do sports often result in aggressive behaviour? And what can be done about it? In this chapter an attempt will be made to shed some light on this perplexing problem. To do so, we must realize that an important step in curbing aggression in sport involves understanding the exact nature of aggression as well as those situations most conducive to violent behaviour. The remainder of this chapter, then, will: (a) require you to develop a specific understanding of the term 'aggression', (b) examine the proposed causes of aggression in sport as well as specific implications for the athlete and coach, and (c) look at specific behavioural interventions with potential to curb the incidence of aggression in sport. Along the way you will be provided with several questions and exercises that will challenge you to examine your personal potential for reducing aggression in your own sport – particularly if you are involved in coaching.

How Do We Define Aggression in Sport?

The term aggression has traditionally been used to refer to a wide range of different behaviour. We use the term when depicting violent outbursts such as fighting, but we also talk about the aggressive player who single mindedly makes a football tackle, and who gives 100 per cent. Further confusion results when we attach value judgements or emotional connotations to the term aggression. For example, some aggressive behaviour is considered good, other behaviour is bad. Also, we are often inconsistent in our value judgements about aggressive behaviour. Thus, it is acceptable to fight in some situations, but not in others. These inconsistencies have undoubtedly served to help perpetuate the problem.

In reality, most aggressive behaviour in sport is neither completely good nor completely bad. Instead, aggression is seen as repulsive by some people and completely justifiable by others. Furthermore, the same person often views aggression as acceptable in some situations and not acceptable in others. For this reason, you will find it easier to understand and explain aggression in sport if you do not think of aggression as totally good or bad, positive or negative, but simply as behaviour to be understood.

Certainly, it is easy to label certain kinds of behaviour such as fist fights or kicking an opponent as aggressive. Other behaviour, however, is not so easy to classify. Before continuing this discussion, define what you mean by aggression in sport. Write your answer on a piece of paper and refer back to it at the end of this chapter.

Now consider the following examples:

1.   Two professional boxers fight for a living.
2.   Two hockey players have a fight during a heated contest.
3.   A rugby player shoulder barges an opponent to the ground whilst driving forwards for a try.
4.   An American footballer, having been tackled very hard, retaliates with an illegal elbow.
5.   A track athlete hopes an opponent will get injured.
6.   A baseball player swears at an opponent in a heated moment.
7.   A basketball player, after taking an elbow in the face going for a rebound, swings at the perpetrator but the punch does not land.
8.   A tennis player slams the racket into the ground after missing an easy volley.
9.   A soccer player injures an opponent's shin by accident while going for the ball.

How many of the above examples do you define as aggressive behaviour? Have you excluded those examples that fall outside your own definition? Can legal tactics be defined as aggressive? What if someone tries to hit you but misses? Can aggression be verbal? Does smashing a tennis racket qualify as aggressive behaviour? What is the role of intent in defining aggression? Do negative thoughts represent aggression? Obviously there will be some disagreement between those replying to these questions, but they do point out the difficulty in attempting to define the term aggression in sport.

*Few themes in the sporting context have received as much
attention as that of aggression and violence.*

In spite of the aforementioned difficulties, a reasonable consensus has been reached in sport psychology. The following
definition is offered for consideration. Aggression is any behaviour intended to harm another individual or object by physical or
verbal means.

This raises several key points. First, aggression involves behaviour. Thinking negative thoughts or wanting to hurt someone is
not aggression. Second, aggression involves intent. Accidental
harm does not qualify as aggressive, but acts that are intended
to harm another individual or object are aggressive, regardless
of whether they are successful. And finally, aggression involves
harm or injury. This harm is not limited to physical assaults
but may include verbal acts aimed at embarassing another person. The definition can also include destroying property or
equipment.

In summary, the above definition outlines aggression as we
commonly understand it. One final distinction is useful. Sport
psychology literature consistently differentiates between instrumental and goal aggression. Instrumental aggression encompasses those aggressive acts that are performed to achieve a
non-aggressive goal. Much of sport aggression is instrumental,
and includes tackling hard to win the ball, physical contact to

'box-out' an opponent in basketball, and other forms of physical contact to stop an opponent. These acts are performed as a means towards an end and are considered acceptable in the world of sports. Conversely, some aggressive acts are performed as an end in themselves and are not acceptable. In such cases the goal aggression has harm as its primary aim. Examples include fighting, swearing at an opponent or referee, and any other behaviour aimed at harming another individual or object. It is primarily these types of aggressive acts that must be eliminated.

The remainder of this chapter explores the causes of goal aggression in sport and suggests practical implications for athletes and coaches wishing to curb such undesirable behaviour.

What Causes Aggression in Sport?

Research has uncovered a variety of factors that may be responsible for causing aggression in sport. In the following section we examine the more popular theories and suggest some practical implications for the athlete and/or coach.

Factor 1: Competition

One possible source of aggression in sport involves the very nature of competition. One of the earliest psychological theories developed to explain aggression is called the frustration–aggression hypothesis. Simply stated, this theory suggests that frustration increases the likelihood of aggressive behaviour. Frustration, in this case, is defined as a goal-blocked response. Given this definition, it is readily apparent that competitive sports involve a large number of goal-blocked responses. The loser is obviously frustrated by losing, but both the eventual loser and winner are frustrated throughout the contest by the numerous goal-blocked responses at the hands of the opponent.

Soccer players, for example, are continually frustrated when successfully tackled by an opponent. Tennis players experience frustration after every losing point. Golfers are frustrated when they miss an easy putt. In fact, all sports involve some form of frustration. Therefore, from what we know about the frustration–aggression connection, it seems reasonable to assume that competition may generate aggressive behaviour. Although we cannot change the nature of competition, there are certain things that we can do to lessen the aggression-inducing effects.

IMPLICATION 1A

Some tennis coaches have developed an interesting technique to avoid the build-up of frustration in their players. They emphasize that a tennis match is a series of 'one-point games'. This encourages the player to regard each point as representing the outcome of the match. At the same time it teaches the player to prevent the harmful build-up of frustration. How might this same technique be of value in your own particular sport?

IMPLICATION 1B

A second obvious method involves bringing in a new game strategy. If you are continually being frustrated in your efforts, try a new game plan. Slow down the game, attack a different zone, perhaps use a one-iron instead of a driver. Often athletes (and coaches) miss the obvious and stay with a game plan that is not working. Get used to trying alternative strategies when things are not going as planned. What alternative strategies do you have for your game plan/sport?

IMPLICATION 1C

Finally, evidence is starting to surface that suggests a relationship between fitness and frustration/aggression. While the research is sparse in this area, it seems reasonable to assume that the less fit individual will become frustrated more easily, turning to aggressive responses. By keeping yourself in top shape it should be possible to react more imaginatively within the laws of the game when things get tough. This provides a much better alternative than responding aggressively.

Factor 2: Outcome of the Contest

Research has consistently shown losers to behave more aggressively than winners. The frustration–aggression hypothesis outlined in the previous section is usually used to explain this theory. Since the loser experiences more goal-blocked responses, the athlete becomes more frustrated and acts more aggressively. Closely related to this point, team standing has also been found to be related to the degree of sport aggression.

It appears that teams in the lower standings aggress more than higher ranked teams. Perhaps this is because the lower ranked teams are more frustrated. An alternative explanation may be that these individuals have less to lose. Because they have little or no chance of winning the championship, they resort to aggressive behaviour to act out their frustrations. Either way, this finding has certain implications for the athlete and coach.

IMPLICATION 2A

After a defeat it is important for the coach to debrief the athletes. During this session the coach should positively review their performance. Specific recommendations regarding ways to improve the weaker aspects of the game should be stressed. It is also important to point out that aggressive play will only result in more losses. Remember to stress the importance of technical improvement as a means to get the team back on track. Do you focus on the positive aspects of an unsuccessful performance? What are some specific ideas you may suggest to guard against similar losses in the future?

IMPLICATION 2B

If your team is entrenched in the lower standings, you would be well advised to change your original goal (ie., to win the championship) to a revised, more attainable goal. For example, you may want to establish a new goal, reducing the number of goals/points against per contest, or reduce the number of penalties/fouls per match. This change of focus takes the emphasis off winning and establishes goals that are more attainable. This in turn results in less frustration and concomitantly less aggression. What are some revised, attainable goals that could be implemented in your sport in a similar situation?

Factor 3: Point Spread

Closely related to the preceding factor, the gap in points achieved by opposing teams has consistently been found to relate to the amount of observed aggression. When the score is close or tied, there tends to be less aggression. This is probably because when the score is close, one penalty or foul can determine the outcome of the contest. Under such conditions both coaches and players tend to become more cautious and thus less aggressive. Conversely, when there is a very large discrepancy between scores, more aggressive acts occur. This often happens because the game has become out of reach. When this happens, certain actions can reduce the chances of aggression escalating.

IMPLICATION 3A

When the game is out of reach, this is a good time for the coach to work on a new strategy or play. For example, if the score in a basketball contest is 75–35, this would be a good time to try out a new zone press that you have been working on in practice. Since the outcome has already been determined to all intents and purposes, implementing the new strategy provides athletes with the opportunity to practise the new technique in a real game. This simulation will prove valuable in future contests. It will also reduce the athletes' present frustration level by changing their game focus from winning to practising a new strategy which will decrease the chance of aggressive behaviour. What new strategy or game plan do you have that could be implemented in similar circumstances?

IMPLICATION 3B
Pursuing the preceding point, the coach could utilize a time-out to outline a new goal for the remainder of the contest. Reconsider Implication 2b, where this idea was previously explained. What other examples could you suggest for your sport?

Factor 4: Home v Away Matches and Fan Reaction

Soccer studies have found that visiting teams commit more fouls and play more aggressively than home teams. Some researchers suggest that this could be the result of several factors, including the goading that the home team and fans often display towards their visitors. If your athletes perceive hostile reactions from the crowd, this could increase their arousal level which in turn would result in more aggressive behaviour. Once again, there are certain precautions that can be taken to decrease the chances of play becoming more aggressive in these situations.

IMPLICATION 4A
During a team meeting the coach should remind the athletes of the probable fan reactions to be expected. Stress the importance of sticking to your original game plan and not being goaded into retaliating with fouls or penalties. Point out that the best way to deal with the hostile crowd is to beat their home team. All efforts should be geared toward that end result. How will you mentally prepare your athletes for hostile crowd reactions in the future?

IMPLICATION 4B
As a coach you should become more aware of the latest research in attention control training. Many successful teams are now utilizing this approach. By teaching your athletes how to recognize and correct attentional problems, you will greatly reduce the amount of team aggression during away matches. Several eastern European teams practise accommodation to crowd reactions. They do this by introducing crowd noise on tape recorders into their practice sessions. By manipulating the volume and

content of taped crowd noise, and eventually substituting live accomplice fans in practices, athletes can be desensitized to the negative effects of hostile crowds. How could crowd desensitization training be used in your training programme?

Factor 5: Physical Contact

The degree of physical contact has also been suggested as a motivator of aggressive behaviour. The very nature of some sports (e.g. ice hockey, rugby, and to some extent even basketball) requires a high degree of bodily contact. Often this physical contact results in retaliation, and in some cases aggression escalates to the point of fighting. The reason why this happens is not completely clear. Some people feel that since physical contact is really a type of goal-blocked response, the frustration-aggression hypothesis would explain the increased incidence of aggression resulting from player contact. However, since this contact does not always lead to aggression, other factors must be involved. One such factor is perceived intent, or attribution.

This concept will be examined in the next section. For now, suffice to say that physical contact does appear to be related to an increase in aggressive behaviour in sport. Although we cannot change the nature of certain sports, we can guard against the negative effect of this contact.

IMPLICATION 5A

If you feel your athletes are responding aggressively to physical contact, you may wish to bring in new responses. This entails having your athletes substitute an alternative behaviour for the usual retaliatory behaviour. For example, an agreement could be reached that after every time your athletes are physically checked, they respond with 30 seconds of maximum effort. This alternative behaviour has two primary functions. First, it increases the likelihood of regaining control. And second it substitutes a more functional response to the contact. Techniques of this nature are good preventative measures against aggressive retaliation. Name some ways you could use this technique in your sport.

IMPLICATION 5B

A second very important role of the coach in this regard is to teach 'clean' tackling techniques. It is not unusual for some coaches to endorse tactics that are somewhat less than legal or slightly outside the rules. While this is usually done to gain a small advantage, it often results in open conflict when implemented in a game. Remember, if all coaches taught proper tackling techniques, much needless sports aggression could be eliminated. Are you prepared to take the first step for the good of your sport? Describe some concrete examples of how this might be done with your athletes.

Factor 6: Player Attribution

An area of social psychology known as attribution theory (explained fully in Chapter 5) provides another possible explanation for the incidence of aggression in sport. In simple terms, attribution refers to our perceived causes of an event. Using an example from competitive sport our reaction to physical contact will differ according to how we perceive the act. So a stiff tackle in rugby or American football will be interpreted differently depending upon whether we think the opposing player was trying to deliberately hurt us or gain control of the ball. Specific cues such as the player's reputation, body-language, and verbal follow-up will lead to a specific interpretation. In other words it is not just physical contact, but our interpretation of that contact which determines whether we respond aggressively.

IMPLICATION 6A

It is important for a coach to brief athletes on physical contact. While it is obvious that contact may be an integral part of your sport, interpreting it is not always easy. Remember to reinforce the idea that physical contact is to be used as a means to an end, not as an end in itself. Approaching contact in this manner does not invite retaliation.

By the same token it is sometimes important to prepare your athletes mentally for a competition involving a 'dirty player'. In such cases it is valuable to stress the importance of not being tricked into aggressive retaliation. Point out that this is what your opponent wants. The best way to retaliate is with maximum effort to perform well. Can you think of other suggestions to offer your athletes to avoid aggressive retaliation?

Factor 7: Referees

The referee has also been cited as a possible cause of aggressive behaviour in sport. Anyone doubting the referee's potential to cause aggression has never seen John McEnroe play tennis. On a more serious note, however, if a referee does not rule firmly players soon learn that aggressive play is tolerated. This in turn leads to escalating aggression with players responding increasingly aggressively.

IMPLICATION 7A

The best a coach can do in the situation described is talk to the referee, or instruct your captain to convey your concern. The approach should be low key and non-threatening. Merely express concern that aggressive behaviour is going to increase drastically without firm and fair refereeing. Suggest that it is up to the referee how this is done, and that it was entirely your concern for the athletes that prompted such a request. Then thank the referee. What would you say to a referee in a situation like this?

IMPLICATION 7B

Stress to your athletes that although the referee's actions are beyond control, their own behaviours are not. Reiterate the importance of sticking to your game plan and not getting lured into retaliatory aggression. What other suggestions might you offer your athletes?

Factor 8: Coaches and Parents

Both coaches and parents have been found responsible for prompting aggressive behaviour in sport. This comes as no surprise when one considers that these individuals are in the closest and most frequent contact with the athlete. However, in all fairness to these individuals it is unlikely they realize the harm they are doing. While it is always possible to find an isolated example where a coach or parent intentionally instructs a player to aggress, situations of this nature are in the minority. More often than not the influence is far more subtle. The best way to explain what happens is by reference to the psychological term 'reinforcers'.

Generally speaking, a reinforcer is anything that happens after a specific piece of behaviour that changes the probability of the same behaviour re-occurring. Reinforcers can be either positive or negative. Positive reinforcers cause us to repeat the same behaviour in the future, while negative reinforcers have the opposite effect. In other words, if a player behaves aggressively and receives a positive reinforcer (e.g. praise from teammates), then this greatly increases the chances that the athlete will behave aggressively again when an appropriate situation presents itself. In contrast, if the aggressive act is followed by a negative reinforcer (e.g. criticism from the coach), then the aggressive behaviour is less likely to be repeated.

It is important to realize that there are many types of reinforcers that operate in sport. These different types of reinforcers are summarized in **Figure 13**.

IMPLICATION 8A

In order to control aggression in sport, parents and coaches must have a thorough understanding of the various types of reinforcers that occur in sport. We have already pointed out that parents and coaches are not always aware they are providing these reinforcers, let alone their effect on subsequent aggressive behaviour. To increase your self-awareness of this issue, complete **Exercise 9**. This will not only help you identify situations where you have unconsciously added to the problem, but will also require you to identify reinforcing strategies with potential to reduce aggressive behaviour in your sport.

Exercise 9

This exercise asks you to identify any occasions where you have unintentionally provided a positive reinforcer to your athlete for aggressive behaviour. Suggest a more appropriate response. Remember, this exercise will be of value only if you are honest.

Ways I have positively reinforced aggressive behaviour	A more appropriate response at that time would have been to . . .

Note: Have you included different types of reinforcers in your analysis?

How many times have you been unconsciously adding to the problem? Do you now feel better equipped to start curbing aggression in your athletes?

IMPLICATION 8B

Since positive reinforcers increase the likelihood of a certain kind of behaviour happening again, ensure you positively reinforce non-aggressive behaviour. Statements such as 'Well done, Bill, you sure made that guy look silly by walking away', or 'I'm really proud of you, Suzi – you gave 100 per cent on that effort' create a climate for non-aggressive play. By showing your athletes that non-aggressive play will be rewarded, you increase the likelihood

Type of reinforcer and description.	Examples of reinforcers that increase aggression.	Examples of reinforcers that decrease aggression.
Social reinforcers: Verbal or non-verbal social behaviour.	Approval, encouragement, praise, attention for aggressive behaviour. 'Well done, Bill. You sure thumped him good.' 'Come over here, and tell me what it felt like to knock him down like that.'	Disapproval, reproof, degradation, withdrawal of attention resulting from aggressive behaviour. 'That was really stupid, getting in a fight, Bob.' 'I don't even want to be associated with such a dirty player.'
Performance reinforcers: a) Intrinsic: the natural feedback from a response. b) Artificial: performance-related information from the coach, teacher, or teammates.	a) The 'feeling' of landing a punch. The bodily sensations of being in a fight. b) 'Next time you're in that position, hit him back.' 'If he does that to you again, give him an elbow in the mouth.'	a) The 'feeling' of an alternative behaviour, such as a perfectly executed pass. The bodily sensations of scoring a basket rather than roughing it up. b) 'Next time you're in that position and retaliate with a cheap shot, I'm going to sub you for the rest of the game.'
Internal reinforcers: a) Self-control: personal reasons for acting a certain way, internal motivation. b) Vicarious: viewing other people's behaviour and the resulting consequences.	a) 'If I don't fight back, my teammates and the spectators will think I am a coward.' b) Watching fans, teammates, parents, and coaches getting excited about witnessing a fight or dirty play. 'Boy, the fans sure got behind Mary after she knocked that girl down with an elbow.'	a) 'If I fight, my parents will yell at me and the coach will sub me.' b) Watching fans, teammates, parents and coaches disapprove of fighting or dirty play. 'People sure seemed disgusted with Mary after she threw that elbow.'
Material reinforcers: Tangible rewards such as money, prizes, badges, or sweets.	'Come on Andy, I'll buy you a pizza. I was sure proud of the way you stood up for yourself in that fight.'	'Come on Andy, let's get that pizza I promised you if you could go two games without taking a roughing penalty.'
Token reinforcers: Material or symbolic reinforcers that can be exchanged for another reinforcer of greater value.	'You've earned your five points for going out there and roughing it up like the way I told you. Here's that autographed ball you wanted.'	'Give me those five tokens you earned for completing five games without a penalty. In exchange, here's a ticket to that show you wanted to see.'

Fig 13   Summary of reinforcers that control aggressive behaviour in sport.

that aggressive behaviour will decrease. Name some types of non-aggressive behaviour in your sport that deserve positive reinforcers.

Factor 9: Observing Aggressive Behaviour

Although this factor is covered under internal reinforcers (**Figure 13**), it is so widely quoted that it deserves some additional consideration. A great deal of research has been conducted that indicates the mere viewing of an aggressive model can lead to increased aggressive behaviour by the viewer.

Psychologists suggest three possible causes for this occurrence: (a) viewing aggression may result in the observer learning new aggressive responses, (b) viewing aggression may result in a dislike of aggressive behaviour, and (c) seeing aggression may facilitate previously learned aggressive acts. Regardless of the mechanism, it seems reasonable to conclude that observing aggressive sport behaviour will lead to future aggression. The problem of viewing aggression is compounded by the tremendous TV exposure of sport. When one considers how much time the average child spends watching TV and how sport continually takes up more TV time, serious implications arise. There are, however, certain steps that can help reduce any negative effects.

IMPLICATION 9A
We have already discussed the role of reinforcers in aggression control. Take a few minutes and review **Figure 13**. By using negative reinforcers to interpret observed aggression in an unfavourable manner, your athletes will vicariously learn that aggression is undesirable and will not be tolerated in your sport. Suppose you and your team are watching another contest and a fight breaks out. What would you say to portray aggression in a negative light?

Aggression and Your Sport

Any number or combination of the previous factors may operate at any one time. Although we have looked at specific examples and implications, it is important that you target those factors that are most prevalent in your sport. It is also crucial that you develop specific strategies to reduce aggressive behaviour in your athletes. Take whatever time you need and complete **Exercise 10**. This analysis highlights the importance of the discussion to date. It will also provide you with a working blueprint for aggression control.

Self-Control of Aggression

So far we have focused almost exclusively on what the coach can do to better understand and control aggression. In the final analysis, however, it is the athlete who must control aggressive tendencies. It is therefore important to examine techniques that can be used by the athlete.

Exercise 10

This exercise asks you to identify the factors responsible for aggressive behaviour in your own sport. It also asks you to identify specific strategies to deal with each of the problem areas.

Factors most responsible for aggression in my sport.	Specific strategies for dealing with this factor.

Note: Have you developed more than one strategy for each factor?

The field of psychology has developed certain behaviour therapy techniques that have special relevance for curbing aggressive behaviour in sport. The following section will examine two specific behavioural self-control strategies that will help an athlete eliminate or cut down on aggressive behaviour.

The Contract

Psychological research has consistently found that the use of behavioural contracts is very effective in changing a wide range of behaviour. The self-control contract is a document that should be designed by the coach and athlete. In its simplest form the contract includes (a) a specific definition of the behaviour you are trying to eliminate, (b) punishment for not completing the contract, (c) reward (positive reinforcer) for successful completion of the contract, (d) the contract partners, (e) the date, and (f) signatures of both parties. To give you some practice at this procedure, you are asked to complete **Exercise 11**. To guide you, a sample contract is included.

Although the contract is mutually developed by the coach and athlete, it is important to remember that the athlete is ultimately in charge of the behaviour.

Response Prevention Training

Another self-control strategy involves developing a plan to deal with problem situations. This technique, known as response prevention training, involves (a) identifying those situations that have often led to aggression in the past, and (b) developing specific alternative strategies that will help you avoid behaving aggressively. For example, an individual who usually reacts aggressively as a result of hostile spectators can develop a plan to deal with situations of this nature. The most common way of accomplishing this is using positive self-statements. In utilizing this technique, there are three specific time intervals that must be considered.

Preparation phase

Before the competition the athlete trys to reduce the tendency to aggress in two ways. First, the performer should emphasize the impersonal rather than personal nature of competition. Second, positive self-statements are substituted for negative thoughts. Using our previous example, the athlete develops self-statements such as 'the crowd is not against me personally, they just want their team to win', and 'I know I play better if I keep my cool'. These and similar statements help the athlete prepare for the inevitable provocation.

Impact phase

This occurs when the performer hears the negative crowd reaction, and counters with repeated positive self-statements such as 'I'm calm and I'm not going to let the crowd bother me', and 'I'll do well if I maintain control'.

Exercise 11

Using the sample contract as a guideline, you are asked to identify a specific form of aggressive behaviour you would like to curb in one of your athletes. Then write out a proposed self-control contract. Remember to include all of the elements of a contract listed previously.

Aggression Self-Control Contract
(Sample)

I, Bugsy Brown, agree to stop verbally abusing my opponents during competition. For completing five matches without an incident of this nature, I will treat myself to the new record I want. For each incident of verbal abuse I perform, I agree to be benched for the same number of following matches. Also, I will not allow myself to buy the record for at least one month.

This agreement is entered into between Bugsy Brown and John Counsellor, and dated July 1, 1991.

Signed (Athlete)	Signed (Coach)

Aggression Self-Control Contract
(Exercise)

Note: Have you included all of the necessary components of a contract?

Reflection phase

After successfully avoiding an aggressive confrontation, the athlete should administer the self-reward of a mental pat on the back, such as 'Well done, you didn't let the crowd get to you this time', and 'See, you do play better when you keep control'.

With proper planning by the coach and co-operation by the player, these techniques can go a long way in helping the athlete control any tendencies. To familiarize yourself with this

Exercise 12

Using the sample worksheet as a guideline, you are asked to identify those situations that have often resulted in aggression in the past, and develop self-statements to encourage alternate responses.

Aggression Response Prevention Worksheet
(Sample)

Provocation to aggression	Phase	Self-statements
Hostile crowd reaction	Preparation	'The crowd is not against me personally – they just want their team to win.' 'I know I play better if I keep cool.'
	Impact	'I'm calm and I'm not going to let the crowd get to me.' 'I know I can do well if I maintain control.'
	Reflection	'Well done, you didn't let the crowd get to you this time.' 'See, I do play better when I keep control.'

Aggression Response Prevention Worksheet
(Exercise)

Provocation to aggression	Phase	Self-statements

Note: These techniques must be practised on a regular basis.

technique, complete **Exercise 12**. As a guideline the previous examples are included on a summary worksheet.

Conclusion

This chapter has examined a wide range of factors that are responsible for aggression in sport. In reviewing these different theories, you have been constantly challenged to work with the material as it relates to your own particular sport. It is hoped that these frequent questions and exercises have helped you to develop an observable and workable approach to curbing aggressive behaviour in sport. Finally, the chapter concludes by 'putting the ball in the athlete's court'. Specific behaviour self-control techniques were offered for your consideration. By taking the time to familiarize athletes with these strategies, coaches will be going a long way in reducing the incidence of unwanted aggression in sport.

CHAPTER FIVE

Interpreting Success and Failure
Dr Stuart Biddle

As an introduction to this chapter, complete **Exercise 13**.

Exercise 13

Think of the following situations in sport. You . . .

1. play well, but lose to a superior opponent.
2. play well and win against a tough opponent.
3. play badly but still manage to win against a weak opponent.
4. play badly and lose to an opponent you know you can beat.

In which of these would you feel (a) most satisfied and (b) least satisfied.

This chapter will outline what we currently know about the way athletes and coaches think about success and failure in sport. It will also describe the reasons we give for our successes and failures in sport, the possible consequences of stating these reasons, and the different ways people think about 'success'. With a knowledge of this information athletes will better understand their motivation.

Reasons People Give for Success and Failure

Here are some common reasons given by athletes after a success:

'I really played well today; that training is paying off!'
'I think I've got a natural talent for running – it seems to come quite easily to me.'
'I tried like mad in the final set, and that's what pulled me through.'
'Phew! I was lucky to get away with that one!'

Now consider some reasons people may give for failing in sport:

'I played like an idiot! I deserved to lose.'
'I can't play this game – it's impossible.'
'I was really lazy today – I couldn't get going at all.'
'I thought I was unlucky to lose that one!'

These are the reasons athletes often give for a performance, whether good or bad. In effect such statements are attributions and the earliest relevant research was carried out in schools and universities. Researchers asked students why they thought they had passed or failed an examination. Four common factors emerged: ability (I am/am not intelligent); effort (I did/did not study hard); difficulty of the task (the exam was easy/difficult); and luck (I was lucky/unlucky). Although other attributions were also found these four emerged as the most important and frequent. For some time, sport psychologists used these same four attributions when questioning athletes. For example, after losing a match a player might be asked 'to what extent was your loss due to your lack of ability?' These studies nearly always compared winners with losers.

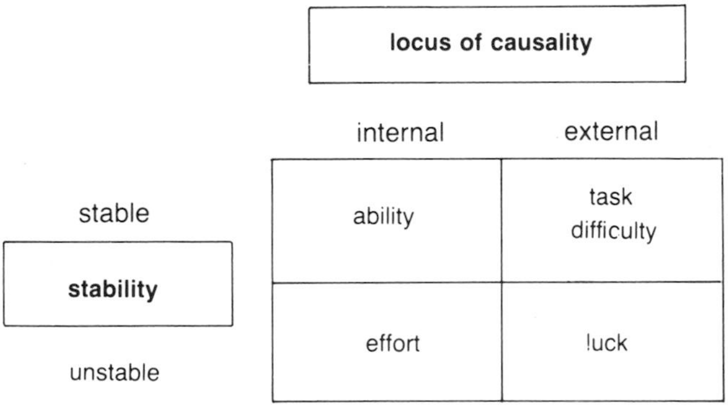

	locus of causality	
	internal	external
stable	ability	task difficulty
stability		
unstable	effort	luck

Fig 14   An early model of attributions and dimensions.

Winners usually gave attributions that referred to themselves, such as 'I won because I tried hard.' Losers tended to give a mixture of personal attributions ('I lost because I was lazy') and attributions related to nonpersonal factors ('The referee was blind!'). In other words, winners tended to take the credit for their success whereas losers tended to make attributions that partly reflected aspects of the game that were beyond their control, and protected their egos. This winner-loser difference has been referred to as a self-serving bias because it helps winners feel good and losers feel not quite so bad.

Some of the attributions given in sport and school were thought to have common properties. For example, effort and ability refer to the individual, whereas luck and difficulty are linked with specific situations. This approach led researchers to distinguish between the locus of causality dimension – attributions either related to the individual ('internal') or the environment ('external');· and the stability dimension – attributions reflecting something stable and permanent (stable) or the unstable and variable (unstable). This classification is depicted in **Figure 14**.

As you can see, this figure gives a four-way classification of attributions: internal/stable, internal/unstable, external/stable and external/unstable. Also, it shows how attributions were classified after the studies on examinations, not sport. Therefore, the difficulty of the examination was seen to be external (caused by the teacher rather than the individual) and stable (unlikely to change given a similar course in the future). However, is this true in sport? Probably not, as the difficulty (strength) of your opponent is likely to vary from one game to the next, thus making 'task difficulty' external but unstable.

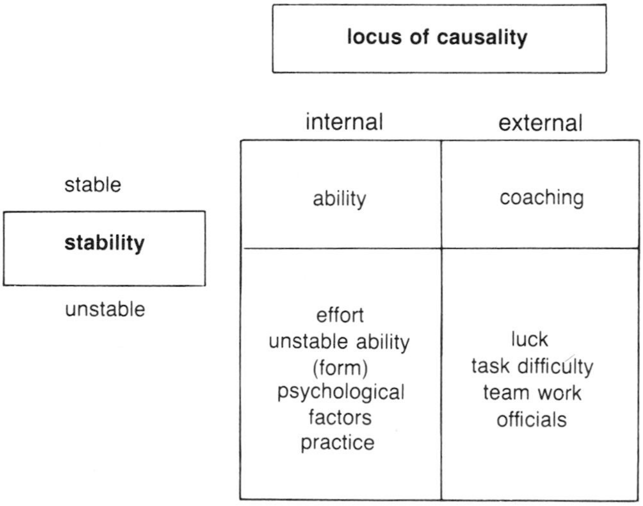

	locus of causality	
	internal	external
stable	ability	coaching
stability		
unstable	effort unstable ability (form) psychological factors practice	luck task difficulty team work officials

Fig 15   A sport-specific model of attributions.

This kind of reasoning led sport psychologists Glyn Roberts and Debbie Pascuzzi from the University of Illinois to question whether the attributions given for examination performance were the same as in sport. They asked 349 university students to respond to a questionnaire in which a particular sporting situation was outlined with the student giving a likely attribution.

The questions were varied in terms of winning and losing, individual and team sports, and the player and spectator.

Overall, the results showed that the attributions of ability, effort, task difficulty and luck were used less than half of the time. Additional attributions used included practice, psychological factors, and match officials. However, these researchers did think that the locus of causality/stability model could still be used, and this is shown in **Figure 15**.

My own view is that attributions in sport will be different and more numerous than this. Even so, the basic attribution dimensions may be the same for both situations.

When do we Make Attributions in Sport?

Although sport psychology researchers have found that winners and losers may differ in the type of attributions they make, do we make attributions after every competition? Look in the newspapers and you should find countless instances of athletes attempting to justify their performance. For example, Arantxa Sanchez Vicario, the Spanish tennis player who won the French Open championships in 1989, said, after her 6–1 6–0 loss against Steffi Graf in 1990, 'every time I hit a winner, she hit it the other way – harder!' Although there is an element of humour here, Arantxa was suggesting that her opponent was just too good on the day. This is a task difficulty type of attribution.

At this stage it is necessary to bring in the Californian psychologist Bernard Weiner who has suggested that attributions are made in real-life situations and not just when a researcher asks you to fill in a questionnaire. He reports different methods to back up his claim. He looked at written reports, such as newspaper articles, and he examined transcripts of various conversations. In both cases he concluded that attributions do occur as part of our everyday thinking. For example, one study looked at sports reports in newspapers and found 594 attributional statements in 107 articles (i.e. 5 per item), while another study found even more attributional statements: 2,269 in 176 articles – nearly 13 per article! Similar results have been found in politics. The conclusion is that attributions are more likely under the following conditions. First when an event was unexpected – for example, it seems more logical that the manager of a soccer team will want an explanation for a surprise loss rather than a predictable win. And second, when one fails to attain a specific goal.

Factors Leading to Specific Attributions

It is possible to identify why certain attributions are made in preference to others. The major factors thought to influence the making of specific attributions are shown in **Figure 16**.

Attribution	Sources of information
Ability	Previous successes and failures. Level of difficulty of task or opponent.
Effort	Self-improvement. Persistence required. Highly valued goal.
Luck	Unique outcome. Randomness of outcome.

Fig 16   Possible sources of information leading to specific attributions.

One very important source of information resulting in particular attributions being made is the coach. For example, the competitor may lose a game and be told by the coach laziness and lack of effort were the causes. However, the player may have thought that the opponent's better tactics were the cause. This is a situation of attributional conflict between player and coach. The chance of this happening can be reduced if the coach allows the player to explain why the game was lost. Then the coach can analyse the situation with more tact and flexibility. This is particularly important because attributions have been found to have some important implications for the way athletes feel about results, motivation, and whether they can improve.

Attributions and Expectations

One of the cornerstones of good coaching is the development of confidence in athletes. Some coaches believe that success breeds success and hence confidence becomes self-generating. To a certain extent this is true. However, it is not necessarily so. Although success is important for the development of confidence, it is also important to consider how your athletes think about, or interpret, success. In other words, attributions can have implications for the development of confidence.

The extent to which the attributions are stable or unstable is the central issue. Take two examples:

1.   'I was really lucky in winning that last game.' [attribution: *unstable*];
2.   'I know that my technique is sound after all that practice.' [attribution: *stable*].

These two statements differ in terms of their stability. Luck (No.1) is usually seen as unstable – you would not expect it to be predictable or permanent. The second statement refers to something more stable and permanent – well-developed skills and technique. These two statements are likely to lead to different expectations about future performance (and hence confidence). No.2 will increase the expectation that success will occur in the future (at least on a similar task), whereas No.1 gives less hope that victory can be repeated since it was due to good fortune. The same logic applies to attributions for failure. Attributing failure to poor skill and technique suggests that failure might occur in the future – hence confidence will be damaged.

In summary, attributions to stable factors give clearer indications of future expectations and confidence. Attributing success to stable factors leads to increased confidence, while attributing failure to unstable factors may (depending on other factors to be discussed later) help reduce the chance of a loss in confidence. **Figure 17** illustrates a positive confidence cycle based on this approach.

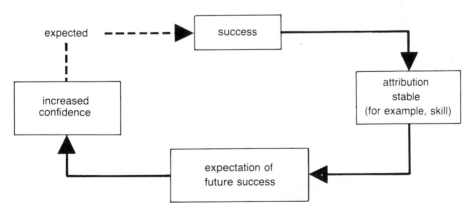

Fig 17   A positive confidence cycle based on stable attributions for success.

Attributions and Feelings

In addition to the potential to affect confidence through expectations, attributions can also be associated with the way we feel about the outcome of a sports contest.

Exercise 14

Think of a time when you had a sporting success. Try to recall the event in as much detail as possible and then write about it. What was the event? What was the outcome? And what *caused* the success? Now try to remember how you felt. Provide three emotions that best describe your feelings.

1. -----------------------------------

2. -----------------------------------

3. -----------------------------------

This exercise is very similar to another study conducted by Dr Weiner. He was interested in whether emotional reactions to achievement events (e.g. sports, examinations, etc) were related to the attributions concerning the outcome.

This research revealed that some emotions are related to the outcome rather than the attribution. In other words, you may feel pleased or satisfied simply because you won, regardless of why you thought you won. This is the initial (or primary) appraisal – the immediate positive/negative reaction common in sport. Dr Weiner referred to this as 'outcome-dependent emotion'. Our own research suggests that the more important you think it is to do well in the event the greater will be the negative reaction after failure. The reverse is not necessarily true for success, however.

In addition to this initial reaction, Dr Weiner also found that particular attributions can lead to particular emotional feelings, or 'attribution-dependent emotions'. **Figure 18** summarizes some typical examples of attribution-emotion links in sport.

If you re-examine **Figures 14** and **15** you will recall the categorization of attributions divides into dimensions: locus of causality (internal/external) and stability (stable/unstable). As far as emotional reactions in sport are concerned it appears that the locus of causality dimension is the important point.

The initial research on attributions stated that the relationship between internal/external attributions and emotions was as follows: internal attributions would strengthen emotional feeling, and external attributions would weaken emotional feeling. This is logical since success attributed to ourselves (internal) will make us feel more positive than if we attribute it to other factors. Similarly, attributing failure to ourselves will strengthen feelings of disappointment and guilt, etc. However, this suggested relationship between locus of causality and emotion is rather too simplistic, although it does provide a good place to start understanding the basic attribution-emotion link.

Attribution	Possible emotional feeling
Success	
Ability	Confidence, competence.
Effort	Pride, gratified.
Mood	Good.
Luck	Surprised, relieved.
Failure	
Ability	Dissatisfied, incompetent.
Effort	Unhappy.
Task difficulty	Depressed.

Fig 18   Examples of links between attributions and emotions.

More recent research has shown that emotions related to self-esteem are more likely to be generated when it is important to do well in sport, and when the outcome is attributed internally. It makes sense that feelings of pride, for example, are related to your own efforts when it is important to do well. Similarly, it has been suggested that social emotions are related to feelings of control over events. For example, feeling guilty about losing a game is much more likely to occur when the loss is attributed to your own lack of effort (a controllable factor) rather than, say, a good opponent. Coaches are more likely to help participants who try hard rather than those who are naturally gifted but lazy. The reason for this is that the social emotions of pity, guilt, anger, etc, are generated by such attributional thinking.

It is also possible that the stable/unstable distinction is important in sports emotion, particularly for time-related emotions. For example, feelings of hope and fear may be related to whether you feel you can succeed in the future. This can be related to stable and unstable attributions.

A summary of some of the possible links between attributions and emotions in sport is given in **Figure 19**.

One of the most important implications of this information concerns how people react to failure in sport since failure has the potential to depress motivation, even to the point of the individual withdrawing from the sport altogether. Before we can understand this problem more fully, it is necessary to discuss the different ways people may view sporting success and failure.

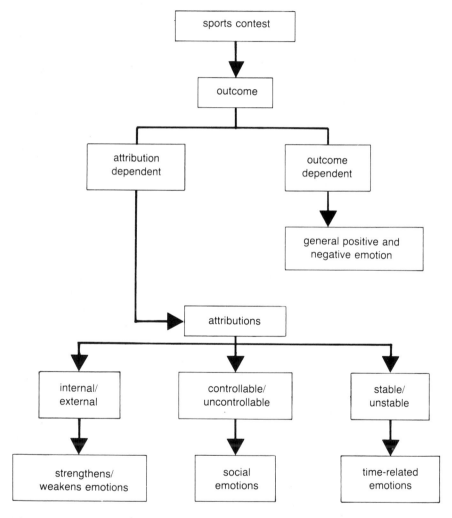

Fig 19   Attributions and emotions in sport.

Attitudes to Performance

'I just want my players to feel successful' is a very common expression heard from coaches. However, what individuals

Attributions have important implications for our motivation in sport, and whether we recover from situations of failure or not.

actually mean by success and failure will vary. Take the example of someone who has just run a first marathon. The pride in achievement will be evident, but might be spoilt by asking 'What was your time?' In other words one view of success is linked to the stop watch, another to the fact of completion.

The study of definitions of sporting success has developed around research focused on the goals (or goal orientations) of individuals. Researchers have attempted to identify exactly what people strive for. They identified the following three goals: mastery (task); ego (ability); and social approval goals.

Mastery or task goals are those associated with self-improvement – a good performance for its own sake. Ego or ability goals are associated with demonstrating high ability and performing better than rivals. In short, sports competitors with an ego-oriented goal are concerned with *proving* their ability, whereas those with a mastery-oriented goal want to *improve* their ability or performance. The social approval goal is when people wish to perform well to please others, such as parents and/or a coach. Younger children in sport are thought to be strongly motivated in this way.

Of course participants in sport are not solely motivated by ego- or mastery-goals. They are likely to be motivated by both, although some individuals may be biased more towards one than another. When Linford Christie won the silver medal in the 1988 Olympic 100m race he said afterwards that he certainly ran to win (and thought he could), suggesting that he was ego-oriented. However, he also expressed delight at beating his own personal best and becoming the first European to run the distance in under 10 seconds, suggesting task/mastery orientation as well.

Goals and Attributions

There is a relationship between sporting goals and attributions. Athletes motivated by ego-orientation, where winning is all-important, will tend to focus on attributions linked to ability. Success will be attributed to high ability, but failure, particularly if repeated, may be attributed to lack of ability. This can be a very damaging strategy, as will be explained later. Those motivated by a mastery goal are more likely to focus on effort attributions since they are interested in self-improvement. This can often be brought about by trying harder, being persistent, or switching strategies, and these require personal effort.

Research by Dr Carol Dweck and her colleagues in America has shown that attributions and motivation can be affected by these different goals. In a study of young children in the classroom she created a situation where the children were presented with a challenging task to complete, but where the mastery goal-orientation (self-improvement) was emphasized. These children displayed high effort and perservered at the task. However, when they were given a similar task with an ego-involved orientation, the results were dependent on the children's own perceptions of how good they thought they were (termed perceived ability).

The children high in perceived ability performed well and were persistent. However, they rejected the chance to improve their skills if it involved exposing themselves to making mistakes in public. The children low in perceived ability responded badly to the task and, when given feedback about their mistakes, attributed their failure to low ability, showed negative emotional reactions, and soon gave up. This is summarized in **Figure 20**.

It appeared from this (and one would expect similar results in sport), that the mastery-goal situation was favourable for motivation and the children tried hard to improve. However, when the situation involved demonstrating high ability (a more competitive situation), only the children with high perceptions of their ability did well. The other children, with perceptions of low ability, displayed a negative response, sometimes characterized by what has been called 'learned helplessness'.

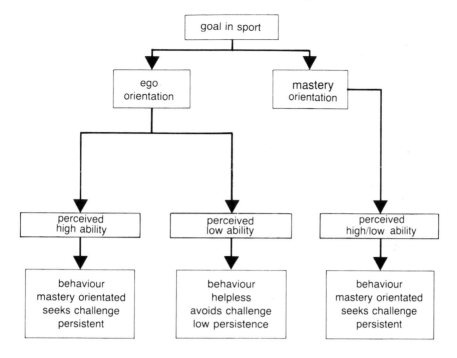

Fig 20   *Goal orientations and sport behaviour.*

Attributions and Reactions to Failure

In the 1960s a number of experiments were conducted investigating the ability of animals to learn. One such experiment placed animals in a maze in which there was no escape. In order to prompt the animals to move a mild electric shock was given. However, the animals soon realized that escape was not possible. When the same animals were then placed in another maze where escape was possible, they failed to seek a way out and were apathetic. The researchers concluded that the animals had learned that their initial response failed to produce a successful outcome and gave up. It was thought that the animals had learned to be helpless – hence the term 'learned helplessness'.

To start with, learned helplessness (LH) was explained by the lack of connection between initial behaviour (trying to escape from the maze) and the outcome (escaping). Humans display this feeling when they express the view 'what's the point – it won't work'. However, work on LH in humans suggested that LH was slightly more complex than a lack of a response-outcome relationship. They linked LH with attributions for failure so that

LH was thought to be more likely to develop when failure was attributed to:

1.   Internal factors (increasing self-blame and negative emotion).
2.   Stable factors (failure is not viewed as changeabie).
3.   'Global' factors (the sense of LH becomes a general problem).

Attribution Retraining

One way of helping athletes avoid the failure – LH downward spiral is by helping players make the most positive attributions they can, especially when they have failed and are more likely to be negative. Some sport psychologists have tried changing the attributions people make, which is known as attribution retraining.

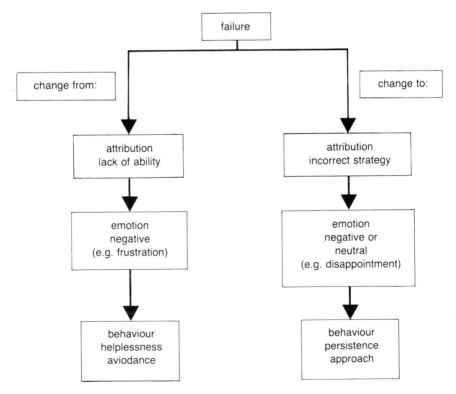

Fig 21   Attribution retraining sequences.

Dr Dweck demonstrated the importance of attribution retraining in an experiment with classroom children. She had one group experience repeated failure followed by a period of success, while another group experienced failure but then had a period of attribution retraining. The attributions for failure due to lack of ability were altered to lack of effort attributions. The results showed that the best recovery from failure was by the attribution retraining group and not the successful group. This was explained by the success group attributing their results to the ease of the task and hence dismissing their success as being out of their control and contrived. However, by restructuring the attributions the other group felt more in control and could see a way of improving their performance. **Figure 21** shows an attribution retraining sequence.

In summary, therefore, attributions can be important in many different ways in relation to failure:

1. They can determine whether LH occurs.
2. They can result from different goal orientations and have implications for reactions to failure.
3. They can be used to help recover from failure through the use of attribution retraining techniques.

Conclusions

Interpreting success and failure in sport is not quite so simple as one might at first think. However, its importance lies in the way we think about success (goal orientations). Also, the way we appraise results (attributions) has implications for emotion, expectations and confidence, motivation, and behaviour.

CHAPTER SIX

Mental
Preparation for
Competition

Brian Miller

An athlete qualifying for an Olympic Final competes against athletes who are fit, strong, flexible, powerful and skilful. All the competitors have devoted time and energy to becoming top-class athletes. However, there is only one champion and two medal winners. Often, the difference between a medal and eighth place is a fraction of a second or a few centimetres. Interviews with athletes who succeed at this highest level often focus on which aspect of their preparation made them different from everyone else. Nine times out of ten these great athletes refer to a mental 'edge', or psychological toughness.

An athlete who wants to compete against other talented athletes needs to think carefully about mental preparation. It is not enough to expect to win simply because you have covered more mileage than the next athlete, or because you have lifted heavier weights. In the final analysis, it is often more important to keep your head in the pressurized environment of competition.

This chapter offers clues and advice as to how you might approach a competition. The suggestions have been tried and tested by athletes at all levels in a variety of sports, and have helped competitors to achieve a degree of consistency in their performance. The skills are not a magic wand though, and they do not guarantee success. However, if you apply yourself to this aspect of your preparation you will reduce the chances of 'choking' or underachieving on the big day.

The Success Cycle

Research into the psychology of sport has shown that performance is based around something called the success cycle. The cycle shows the relationship between how you feel about yourself and how you are likely to perform in competition.

If you have a positive self-image, you are more likely to have a positive attitude which in turn is likely to lead to higher expectations. This usually leads to improved behaviour (going to bed a little earlier or spending more time on preparation), and with these improvements the level of performance increases. Consequently, your self-image is enhanced and matters progress well.

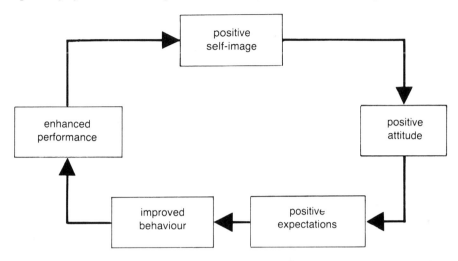

Fig 22   The success cycle.

However, the effects of a negative self-image can be just as powerful, so it is important that you learn to keep the cycle moving upwards rather than downwards. The easiest way to ensure this happens is by ensuring you are getting the most out of all training sessions and competitions. One way of making sure this happens is by setting yourself goals and targets.

We know that preparation is the key to success. A Texas oil billionaire once said that there are three secrets to success. First, individuals have to work out exactly what they want from a certain situation – not roughly or vaguely, but specifically. Then they have to work out what costs or sacrifices would be needed to get these things. Finally, they have to be prepared to pay those costs and make those sacrifices. Unfortunately, many athletes get two out of three right, but fail to get the hat-trick.

Competition preparation is all about establishing habits that lead to success. Canadian research with Olympic athletes suggests that there are some basic 'house-keeping' rules that can help in this area. You should set yourself goals on a daily basis. These might relate to school, work or family commitments, as well as sport. Each training session serves a purpose in your build-up, and it is important that you set a goal on each occasion.

GOAL SETTING FOR TRAINING SESSIONS

Goals: 1

2

| Evaluation: | 1 | 0 | 1 | 2 | 3 | 4 | 5 | 6 | 7 | 8 | 9 | 10 |
| | | Terrible | | | | | | | | | Very good | |

| | 2 | 0 | 1 | 2 | 3 | 4 | 5 | 6 | 7 | 8 | 9 | 10 |
| | | Terrible | | | | | | | | | Very good | |

Comments: ....

GOAL SETTING FOR TRAINING SESSIONS

Goals: 1

2

| Evaluation: | 1 | 0 | 1 | 2 | 3 | 4 | 5 | 6 | 7 | 8 | 9 | 10 |
| | | Terrible | | | | | | | | | Very good | |

| | 2 | 0 | 1 | 2 | 3 | 4 | 5 | 6 | 7 | 8 | 9 | 10 |
| | | Terrible | | | | | | | | | Very good | |

Comments: ....

GOAL SETTING FOR TRAINING SESSIONS

Goals: 1

2

| Evaluation: | 1 | 0 | 1 | 2 | 3 | 4 | 5 | 6 | 7 | 8 | 9 | 10 |
| | | Terrible | | | | | | | | | Very good | |

| | 2 | 0 | 1 | 2 | 3 | 4 | 5 | 6 | 7 | 8 | 9 | 10 |
| | | Terrible | | | | | | | | | Very good | |

Comments: ....

Fig 23 Sample page of a training diary.

The goal might be quantifiable, for instance you might want to run a certain time, or improve your standing long jump, or reduce the number of unforced errors on your forehand. However, the goals could also relate to maintaining your concentration throughout a lengthy training session, or increasing your commitment to the stretching element of the warm-down. In any case, it is important that you set a goal before the start of each training session and then evaluate yourself once the session is over. In some sports, like swimming and running, we spend far more time training than competing, and it is vital that you get the most out of the training sessions. It should never get to the stage that you are simply going through the motions. Once the coach has explained the major points, or the workload for a training session, you should get your 'mind in gear', and focus on the key elements of that session. Perhaps while you are going through the first part of your warm-up, you could set yourself a target for the rest of the workout.

Figure 23 is a sample page of a training diary. I have used this approach with several Olympic champions. For each session, the athlete gets a chance to set two goals. At the end of the session they can review themselves on a scale of 1 to 10, and make any relevant comments. These comments might help to set targets for the next day's training session.

Exercise 15

1. Before you begin the training session get 'switched-on'. Set yourself two goals for the day.
2. Write a key word on the back of your hand which relates to your goals and look at it occasionally during the session.
3. After the session is completed, fill in the form shown in **Figure 23** and assess how well you achieved your goal.

In the past, I have had success with athletes by getting them to use a piece of sticking plaster to remind them of their goals for the training session. Rugby players have written a key word on the plaster (for example, 'concentration' or 're-focus') and then placed this on the back of their hand. During a lull in the sessions or between drills, they have glanced at the plaster and concentrated anew on their goals.

After using this type of system for a while, any athlete should be able to see how work has progressed. This will hopefully help lead to an enhanced self-image and hence contribute to the success cycle. In other words, competition preparation can actually begin a long time before the date of the event itself. As a start at using this mental training technique, use **Exercise 15** to focus your attention during your next training session.

Visualization

Another important aspect of competition preparation is known as visualization, imagery or mental rehearsal. World-class New Zealand marathoner Alison Roe once said, 'I cope with the mental pressure by mentally rehearsing my races, or parts of my races beforehand. I always stress the positive things.' Certainly, back in the 1950s and 1960s, top-class athletes talked about using the imagination to prepare for events. People like four-times Olympic discus champion Al Oerter described picturing himself throwing in a variety of conditions. He would imagine dry circles, wet circles, left-handers' wind, trailing after five rounds, or competing in a hailstorm. Steve Backley, Britain's top javelin thrower, once told me that he copied Oerter's visualization technique when preparing for the major championships. Jack Nicklaus is often quoted as saying that he never takes a shot, in practice or in competition, without first of all seeing that shot in his mind's eye. Former world record holder for the 400m hurdles, David Hemery, has described his mental preparation for the Mexico and Munich Olympiads, and emphasized his commitment to rehearsing mentally the details of his forthcoming event. However, while these performers were using this technique in an intuitive manner, there is now little doubt that formal training in mental rehearsal or visualization techniques can enhance performance.

Basically, visualization is a form of skill training that complements traditional physical practice of skills and movements. Quite simply you can sit in a comfortable chair or lie on a bed, relax, and think about your sport. It sounds too good to be true, but we know from a whole range of international research that the combination of physical and mental practice is the most effective way of refining a skill and preparing for an event. This is particularly true if you are trying to improve an ineffective technique. This situation is almost invariably more difficult than when an athlete is starting from scratch with an entirely new skill.

Visualization works because it helps establish the correct blueprint for success. If athletes become effective at visualization, their brain sends electrical messages to the muscles in the same sequence as if they were actually performing that action. The only difference is that the voltage will not be high enough to make the muscles move. However, when an athlete lies still and mentally rehearses a javelin technique, for example, it is not uncommon to see the muscles in the thighs and shoulders making small involuntary movements.

*Great athletes often refer to a mental edge or psychological
toughness that gave them an advantage.*

Khristo Markov, the 1988 Olympic triple jump champion from Bulgaria, was at pains to stress that much of his victory in Seoul was due to his additional commitment to his mental programme from 1987. Speaking at his victory press conference in Korea, he said that he had worked hard at increasing the number of jumping repetitions per week 'by using my thought. My challenge in Seoul was mental rather than physical, but I was well prepared. I had seen myself jumping in that stadium many times before.'

Australian Olympic hockey champion, Debbie Bowman, scored a vital penalty stroke in the 1988 final against South Korea in Seoul. The goal broke the deadlock and Australia went on to win 2–0 in front of 30,000 partisan Koreans. Debbie had been using a visualization programme for the previous 18 months, and afterwards was quoted as saying, 'I knew exactly what I had to do. I'd seen it a thousand times before. It was automatic. It was like *déjà-vu*.'

Brazilian middle-distance star Joaquim Cruz commented after his victory in the Los Angeles 800m final, 'a day before the race I picture myself winning 100 times. I never give myself the chance to picture myself losing.' While he may not call this strategy visualization, mental rehearsal or imagery, he was using it. He was building confidence and rehearsing a number of tactical ideas without suffering from fatigue.

While some coaches have been teaching versions of visualization for many years, I feel that the practice can be optimized by following a few basic ground rules. There are seven key features that can maximize such training. These points are a summary of some of the latest research data that has been compiled from around the world. They are listed in **Figure 24**.

Athletes who are serious about improving their standard of performance should develop the skill of effectively visualizing the technical and tactical elements of their sport. Having acquired this ability, they can use the strategy whenever and wherever they like. In an Olympic village, for example, most athletes are 'tapering' for the competition and they have relatively little training to do. With excess time on their hands, they may be tempted to over-train, over-eat (the dining halls are often the social centre of a village) or become sporting 'butterflies' who flit around watching a number of sporting events. Such behaviour can interfere with competition preparation. Athletes can be encouraged to utilize their time more effectively by using their visualization drills. In this way they are both helping to pass the time, and also building confidence by 'grooving in' the correct technical blueprint.

1. You should adopt a comfortable position (sitting or lying) prior to the session. Your eyes should be closed, and ideally you should have a relatively quiet room in which to practise.
2. Athletes are conditioned to using a warm-up prior to the start of any physical training session. Continue this theme in a mental training session. Start by spending a few minutes focusing on a slow, steady breathing rate and concentrate on relaxing your mind and body.
3. The mental rehearsal should be seen in the correct time-frame. Usually, slow motion or super-fast speeds are not very useful.
4. You should see the event as you do in real life. Rehearse the scene from an internal perspective – ie, looking through your own eyes. Try not to see the movement as if you were watching yourself on TV. The TV version is acceptable, but in the long term it would be better if you could move on to the internal style.
5. Visualization is a skill that needs practice. If you find it difficult, persevere, as progress is made quickly with regular workouts.
6. Don't leave your visualization sessions to chance. They should have a place in your weekly training schedule. Three or four times a week for about 5–10 minutes would be a good start.
7. Always visualize yourself performing well and positively.

Fig 24   Guidelines for visualization.

Committed athletes of all standards should take a leaf out of Jon Ridgeon's book and start learning the skill of visualization. In 1987 this world-class high hurdler commented that 'at the start I like to control my nervousness by visualizing the race. I go through the perfect race in my mind. I think your performance can be improved if you go through it beforehand.'

Exercise 16

Read through the points in **Figure 24** very carefully. Then find a quiet place and make yourself comfortable. Close your eyes and spend a few minutes getting really relaxed. When you feel ready, begin to visualize yourself competing in your sport. Visualize yourself performing very well and concentrate on how it feels. Concentrate on the feelings in your arms and legs, as well as your emotions and confidence. Continue this visualization for several minutes and then open your eyes again. Repeat this exercise several times per week and vary the content of your visualization. This is an important element of any athlete's mental preparation programme.

Any athlete prepared to devote the time and effort required to learn the technique of visualization can keep 'in-tune' even during the off-season, or when out with illness and injuries. Athletes of all standards can benefit from mental training, but must realize it can take a while before they will feel completely comfortable with the technique.

Coping with Pre-Competition Nerves

Many athletes devote time and effort to their sport, making sacrifices to improve. Often they also make a financial commitment in the hope of a major breakthrough. Despite these good intentions though, and often despite some excellent performances in training or in minor competitions, some athletes fail to live up to their expectations. They under-achieve; in the world of international sport this is often described, quite unfairly, as 'choking'.

Yet why do some athletes seem able to perform consistently well when the pressure is really on, while others never 'quite produce the goods'? Why don't all athletes choke?

In 1984, the Americans hoped that Steve Scott would finally fulfil his potential and obtain a middle-distance gold medal in the Los Angeles Olympics. However, after another disappointment, he said 'the pressure got to me because I allowed it to. There were lots of guys like Carl (Lewis) and Edwin (Moses) who coped with it. The pressure was constant, day after day. Like a tourniquet. The closer it got, the harder it was to relax. Normally, before a race, I'm pretty relaxed'. This world-class athlete under-achieved when it mattered most – the Olympic Games. He choked. While there will always be some variation within any athlete's performances in a season, it is particularly frustrating if they save the worst for the most important competition. Obviously, the physical 'peaking' process has something to do with this, but more realistically it is a psychological factor that leads to the disappointment.

One way that you can reduce this variation in performance at such crucial times is by arming yourself with coping strategies. Certain stress management techniques have already been mentioned in Chapter 3. Such techniques can give you the power to gain some control over your reaction to pressure. If you become distracted or overly hyped-up in the days, hours or even minutes prior to an event, it is important that you get yourself back in the groove as quickly as possible. Some people call it being 'in the zone'. They are referring to the Zone of Optimal Functioning (ZOF).

The ZOF is the state in which athletes feel good and sharp. They are in control of their pre-competition nervousness. They are neither too complacent nor too pumped-up, and are focusing on key technical or tactical factors.

It is important that athletes focus their attention on those things in sport which they can control. There is little point in worrying about other athletes. Prior to her 400m hurdles victory in the Seoul Olympics, Australian Debbie Flintoff-King said, 'I just forget about everyone else. I'm only in control of my lane, so that's where I focus'. In a similar vein, the world champion javelin thrower Fatima Whitbread once said, 'It's easy to be put off by extraneous things like the crowd, so I deliberately adopt tunnel vision. I lock into exactly what I want to do'.

Both of these athletes target their focus in such a way that they can perform well even under intense pressure. They are both highly successful and very single-minded. However, even if athletes know what they are supposed to be thinking about, excessive nervousness still has a habit of making athletes under-achieve. In these instances it is vital that you have a method of coping. The most commonly used techniques normally focus on breathing control.

Centering is a breathing technique originally developed about 2,000 years ago by Tibetan monks. Today, it is the world's most commonly used mental training device.

Centering is basically a technique that can help you to reduce tension prior to, or even during, a competition. It gives athletes control over their bodies and allows them to dictate the level of pre-event excitement.

Athletes who take the time to learn centering can keep the technique as a weapon in their armoury. They do not have to use the skill every time they compete, but they know that it is there if they need it. This can be a great confidence booster, and once again it can help set you on the success cycle.

Normally, if athletes practise centering for about one minute per day (in front of a mirror) for two weeks, they acquire the skill for life. Thereafter, one or two minutes practice per week is all that is needed. Use the technique whenever you feel that your nervousness is a little too high and you want to re-gain control.

Exercise 17

Have a go at the Centering technique by following the instructions in **Figure 25**.

Athletes from all sports can gain from this technique. I have taught it to squash players, racing drivers, golfers, rowers, cricketers, hockey players and track and field athletes. It can be used in between points, shots or deliveries. It can be used when the ball is down the other end of the court or pitch. It can be used while you are waiting for the starter to get things under way. Centering is often the first technique that I teach athletes and many Olympic performers have reported its benefit to me.

1.   Stand comfortably with your feet shoulder-distance apart and your knees slightly flexed.
2.   Relax your neck, arm and shoulder muscles. Smile slightly to reduce the tension in your jaw.
3.   Focus on the movement of your abdominal muscles. Notice your stomach muscles tightening and relaxing.
4.   Take a slow, deep breath using the diaphragm. Notice you are extending your stomach.
5.   Consciously maintain the relaxation in your chest and shoulders. There should be minimal chest movement and absolutely no hunching or raising of the shoulders.
6.   Exhale slowly. Let yourself go. Feel yourself get heavier as all your muscles relax.

inhalation

Fig 25 Centering.

exhalation

Despite the power and usefulness of this control technique it cannot be the complete answer to achieving ZOF. In certain instances athletes need to be more aroused rather than less aroused. In other words, they need to pump-up or energize. There are two standard approaches to athletes feeling they are overly relaxed and not sufficiently excited about a competition. First, there is a mental approach to energizing which simply uses the power of the imagination. I have heard athletes say that they have used the image of standing on top of a medal rostrum, or going to fight for a cause in which they believe in an effort to raise their arousal and get into the ZOF.

A slightly different approach to energizing involves using a physical technique. Successful athletes have often used the rapid contraction and relaxation of small muscle groups. Typically, you might see a tennis player quickly and repeatedly clenching one or both fists. Alternatively, you may see a cricketer who is scoring too slowly suddenly start to chew very quickly and vigorously while batting.

In either instance, mental or physical, athletes are employing techniques that are designed to add a certain spark prior to, or during, an event. While I consider centering to be the most important technique in such instances, I am always careful to teach the pump-up methods as well. Without an energizing skill an athlete is not fully equipped for competition.

Pre-Event Focusing

We should never underestimate the power of our thoughts. As **Figure 26** depicts, it is clear that what we think about and how we interpret situations will often determine our physical reactions to issues and events.

In the last decade sport psychologists have begun to examine the nature of an athlete's self-talk. In other words, they have become increasingly interested in what athletes say, or think, to themselves during the last few hours, minutes or seconds before an event, and indeed during an event.

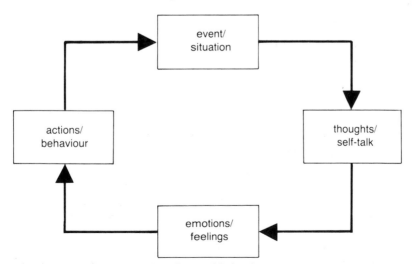

Fig 26 Relationship between thoughts and behaviour.

Anecdotal evidence suggests that top athletes from all sports seem to use certain cues as an aid to their preparation. They seem to focus on the mechanisms that lead to success, rather than success itself. Consider this from a practical point of view. In 1987, Pat Cash won the men's singles at Wimbledon having been helped in his preparation by the Australian sport psychologist, Jeff Bond. Jeff once said that he had to get Pat to ignore the outcome of a given point ('if I get this point, it's the game and then I've won this set', or 'if I don't break his service here, I'll be 5–3 down and then I'm done for') and focus on the process.

The vital process in tennis is to play each ball on its merits. Play one shot at a time. The player should approach the net to volley concentrating on the position of the ball, not that this is an important point to win. The ball does not have a brain, and it does not know that it is 40–15 and 5–3 for the Wimbledon crown!

Fig 27   Pre-event goal setting.

Of course, the aim was still to win, but it was important for Pat not to be distracted by other thoughts and to take care of each shot at a time. That may sound simple, but it really can be quite a difficult system to get right – especially in the big games. Pat Cash was being taught to have what is known as a 'process focus'.

When I work with athletes I like to get them to discuss three levels of pre-event focus – outcome, performance and process. Using an example from a female professional 10-pin bowler, let us examine this aspect of preparation. Her goals are shown in **Figure 27**.

On the tough American circuit this bowler aimed to finish in the Top Ten every week, which was appropriate for her level of skill. She had a performance goal of scoring between 200 and 210 pins per game. Again, this was appropriate and attainable, given her level of skill and experience.

Her process goals were twofold. She used a concentration strategy which focused on one bowl at a time. Having bowled she would evaluate, learn, and then think about her next delivery because the past cannot be changed. Her other process goal was to ensure that her pre-bowl behaviour, or rituals, were consistent. These two process goals were chosen because of her previous experiences on the American circuit. Her goals were worked on in practice sessions, and deemed appropriate by herself and her coach.

Obviously she still wanted to win competitions, but the point is she focused on the process rather than results. Consequently in her second stint on the American circuit she was a regular Top Ten finisher, and she regularly achieved scores of over 200. She had learned that if you take care of the process goals, the performance goals tend to be achieved, and if the performance goals are reached then the outcome goals follow. This really reinforces the point made by Richard Cox in Chapter 2, when he suggested that outcome goals were not the most desirable type on which to focus.

Exercise 18

Using **Figure 27** as a guide, identify a few process goals that you can use in future competitions. Next, practise concentrating on them during a training session and finally, use them in competitions.

Planning for Success

There are many aspects of sport over which we have no control. Team games are plagued by such events as deflections, lucky bounces, strange umpiring decisions or an untimely injury to a key player. Track athletes, golfers and racing sailors can complain about the wind and rain, while cyclists and Formula One drivers are often left to curse the unreliability of their machinery. For as long as humans have been competing in sport, there have always been 'uncontrollables' that have let them down.

As you prepare for a major competition, it is important that you do not become overly upset by these 'uncontrollables', but rather focus your attention on what is controllable. If you can begin a competition thinking 'OK, I've done everything possible to be thoroughly prepared for this event. I've covered every angle, and now, all other things being equal, I'm going to really go for it', then you can exude a certain 'presence' or confidence that is based upon reality.

If, however, you are trying to begin the competition well but are thinking how you wished you had spent more time on checking your equipment or doing your homework on the opposition, then I do not rate your chances of success.

If you have ever had the opportunity to watch world-class gymnasts, basketball players or figure skaters, you may have noticed that they seem to have a consistent approach to their behaviour and performance. If you watch these athletes closely, it becomes apparent that they have a well-learned, consistent routine which they execute each and every time. They seem to do the same things in the same order and with the same timing. If you contrast this with the routines of the inexperienced athlete, you will see many inconsistencies in preparation routines.

It probably makes sense to say that if you want to produce consistent, high-quality performances every time you compete, then you must have a consistent base from which to perform. This involves a consistent skill level, stable tactical appreciation, a steady level of physical fitness, and a set of consistent psychological or behavioural routines. One can probably assume that your specific skills are fairly consistent and that your tactical knowledge does not suddenly decrease overnight. Therefore, poor performances are more likely to be blamed on uncontrollables, or on not handling the pressure, lapses in concentration, not staying focused, etc.

The system I shall describe is known as performance segmenting, and is one way of enhancing psychological control skills. The reason performance segmenting works is that if you have a consistent base from which to perform, you feel more confident, maintain better control over timing, concentration, thought processes, bodily reactions to pressure, and emotional states. If something distracts you from your preparation or concentration during a competition, you will be more likely to recover quickly and refocus on the positive aspects of the task at hand. It is similar to an insurance policy which enables you to remain calm when something goes wrong. Instead of panicking and losing control, you are able to recover quickly from distractions.

To illustrate exactly how the segmenting process works, it is necessary to describe four distinct phases.

Phase 1

You should decide on a definite starting and finishing point for the plan. Some athletes like to begin their plan the night before a competition, whereas others begin on their arrival at the competition venue. In preparation for the Los Angeles and Seoul Olympiads, some athletes planned their entire time in the Olympic village up to and including their events. For these athletes it was important to have a daily plan as part of the controlled preparation for high-quality performances. Obviously, their plans became more precise and detailed as they approached the immediate event, and extremely specific during the course of the event.

Phase 2

Having established the beginning and end of the plan, you should work on a numerical naming system that is not unlike a NASA launch sequence. Almost all athletes who use this system employ the standard – 10, 9, 8, 7, 6, 5, 4, 3, 2, 1, BLAST OFF routine. Some athletes use other systems such as the months of the year (January, February, etc.) but they all have the same sequential quality. From the start to the finish, you should list the parts or segments that are important to you. The number of segments will depend on just how detailed you want the plan to be, and how long a period is to be covered by the plan. **Figure 28** illustrates what a sequence might look like.

10. The night before:
    Prepare equipment bag that you will take tomorrow.
    Shower and relax (listen to music, read).
    Spend 20 minutes relaxing and listening to calming music.
    Go through visualization, imagining yourself performing really
    well tomorrow.

9. About 7.30am.
    Wake up and go for an early morning jog.
    While on the run, start to visualize the competition and rehearse
    your tactics.
    Shower and breakfast.

8. About 9.00 to 10.30am.
    Go through the competition plan and think about a variety of
    'what if . . .' situations. Decide how you will deal with any small
    inconveniencies that occur.
    Listen to your favourite music.

7. 10.30am.
    Go to the competition venue.
    Go to the marshalling area and report in.

6. 11.30am.
    Check your equipment.
    Have a light snack.

5. Approx. 1.00pm.
    Go to the warm-up area and begin with gentle jogging and
    stretching.
    Listen to the day's weather conditions.

4. Approx. 2.00pm.
    Check your arousal level. There's 30 minutes until the time. How
    are you feeling? Do you need to pump up or calm down to be
    getting near that Zone of Optimal Functioning?
    Begin the final phase of your warm-up routine.

3. Approx. 2.10pm.
    Final check of equipment.
    Spend 2–3 minutes visualizing the start of the competition.

2. Approx. 2.20pm.
    Say some positive things to yourself and remind yourself of all the
    work you've put into this event.
    Remind yourself of some of the good performances you have
    recently had.

1. 2.27pm.
    Final check of pre-competition arousal. Use the centering
    technique if required.

BLAST OFF!

Fig 28   Sample pre-event plan.

Phase 3

All athletes will have different priorities concerning what they need to do before an event, and there is no reason why two plans from different athletes should look even remotely similar. The next stage is to implement the draft plan in a mock or low-key event. You need to work to the plan, evaluate it, and then probably fine-tune some of the elements.

Over a period of time you should be getting closer to something that suits you and your needs. You might have more than one plan, depending on the type of competition in which you are involved. As the plan becomes more automatic you should be able to simplify it. For example, perhaps you could replace a sentence with just one cue word. These cue words can be a very effective way of retaining information when the pressure is really on. They can also evoke the correct mental images that you require.

Phase 4

Now you need to record the plan and go about learning it correctly. Nowadays, athletes use a variety of techniques to enhance the learning process. The standard manner used to involve drawing up a series of small hand-held cards that contained the major elements of the plan. These cards went everywhere with the competitor.

Today, with the advent of information technology, athletes are using computers as the means of storing data. They can consistently update their plans and get printouts when they need them. Another common approach is to make an audio-tape recording of the plan. By using a cassette tape and the inevitable personal stereo, you can learn and train at the same time!

Exercise 19

Using **Figure 28** as a guide, make up your own first draft of a pre-event plan. Decide on a particular event or match and then choose a starting point for your sequence. You can then plan out each step leading to the start of the competition.

Obviously, just the learning of a pre-event plan does not make anyone a better athlete! The plan has to implemented, evaluated, refined and tried again. What the segmenting does however, is to focus clearly the mind on what has to be done to achieve consistency. If you are a competitor whose concentration has a habit of drifting prior to an event ('if I win this match, that will . . .') and you often fail to focus on the task at hand, then performance segmenting will probably be very useful. Nevertheless, you still have to score goals, clear hurdles, make tackles, hit winners, etc, but at least you will be controlling everything that can be controlled. Additionally, with this consistent base, you are better prepared to deal with the unexpected events that invariably crop up.

Conclusion

It will be evident from this chapter that mental preparation for competition is not normally something that starts the night before a big event. Rather, it is a general philosophy that should influence almost everything you do in your overall preparation. Preparation is the key to success, and there really are not any short cuts to becoming a champion athlete. When individuals make that all-important transition from being someone who makes promises to someone who makes commitments, then they are likely to fulfil their potential. Until then, the chances of success are limited.

The committed athlete is one who learns the techniques of centering, visualization and performance segmenting. This athlete takes the time and effort to experiment with pre-event focusing, energizing and goal setting for both training and competition. When I address groups of athletes, I often remind them of something that is perhaps a cliché, but none the less very important:

'Remember, the opposition is really the person you see in the mirror every morning. It is that person who tries to persuade you that you do not have to be the model athlete and you can cut corners. Well, if you can win that battle on a daily basis, then you are getting close to finding out just how good you can be in your sport.'

CHAPTER SEVEN

The Psychology of the Coach–Athlete Relationship

Peter Terry

It is sometimes implied that behind every great man is a strong and supportive woman. It could equally be said, with a great deal more certainty, that behind every great athlete moves the guiding hand of a strong and supportive coach. Countless partnerships illustrate this; Linford Christie and Ron Rodden, Daley Thompson and Frank Dick, Sebastian Coe and Peter Coe. There are few relationships in sport more influential or intimate than that between performer and mentor.

Human relationships are complex and the interaction between coach and athlete is no exception. For a coach to translate an athlete's natural talent into consistent performance is a considerable, and at times frustrating, challenge. The challenge might best be summarized as having to clarify and understand their own needs, the needs of the athletes, and the demands of the sport, and then somehow to reconcile and dovetail all three. It would appear to be the blueprint for a complicated juggling act where in reality balls are dropped as often as caught.

The aim of this chapter is to help you understand the nature of coaching from a psychological perspective. It encourages you to clarify your own motives and philosophy towards coaching. It explores the needs of athletes, their differing preferences for coaching, and the differing ways in which they perceive what a coach does. Unfortunately it is not possible to say coach like this and you will be a success, but insight leads to enhanced understanding which in turn increases the probability of you getting it right more often than not.

Understanding the Concept of Coaching

The simplest way of understanding coaching is to view it as an interaction between the coach, the athletes, and the event. The compatability of these three forces will determine outcomes such as how enjoyable the experience is for all concerned, how often a performer wins, and how cohesive a group of athletes become.

The term coach is believed to derive from a 14th-century Hungarian word for a sturdy vehicle designed to carry people over particularly rutted terrain; and so it is that the modern day sports coach has the responsibility of transporting a young athlete on the difficult journey towards athletic maturity and the fulfilment of potential. Along the way a coach may act as teacher or friend, taskmaster or nursemaid, chauffeur or psychologist.

Coaching is, first and foremost, a form of leadership where one person influences and guides others. It involves dealing with people far more than it involves disseminating knowledge and devising state-of-the-art practices. Ideally athletes fulfil their coach's directives because they want to. Good coaches are often charismatic individuals who influence without bullying and gain respect without demanding it. Typically they possess clearly developed philosophies about coaching which are pursued with ceaseless dedication. In the words of Vince Lombardi, one of America's most famous football coaches, to be a success you must 'win the hearts of the people that you coach'.

Unfortunately this is an area where it is easy to lapse into platitudes and to unravel the art of coaching it is necessary to analyse the coach–athlete interaction at a behavioural level: to look at what coaches actually do. The first level of this analysis might be to break down the coaching role into its component parts, to examine the range of skills required, and to list all the functions which coaches are called upon to perform. **Figure 29** illustrates the four fundamental categories of skills which make up the coaching 'pie'.

Technical skills are the basic coaching tools. They are the knowledge-base of a sport, identified by athletes as critical for all coaches, and without which you are in no position to instruct. For instance, a competent tennis coach needs detailed knowledge of how each stroke should be executed, how correct footwork is taught, and how specific drills can be adapted to suit the needs of a particular player.

Tactical skills can be regarded as the analytical and decision-making component of coaching. They are the skills which help win contests. A basketball coach, for instance, must decide which combination of players will be most effective, what play to run, when to substitute and when to call timeouts. The tactical approach of a coach often reflects a general philosophy towards coaching; whether the principle of playing an attacking, exciting style supercedes the safety first approach, and whether the needs of individual performers are sacrificed for the sake of winning.

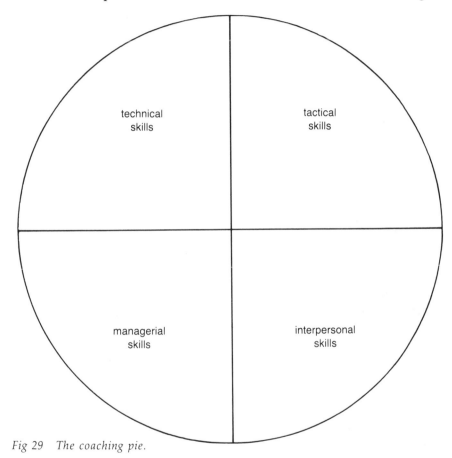

technical
skills

tactical
skills

managerial
skills

interpersonal
skills

Fig 29   The coaching pie.

Managerial skills are required to maintain an organized, systematic approach to coaching. Effective planning, time management and administration have become part and parcel of coaching in modern sports, and coaches overlook them at their peril. A hockey coach may have to deal with league administrators, organize road trips, purchase equipment, keep fitness records, and any number of other managerial tasks which may be perceived as unwanted burdens. There is often, however, a

powerful knock-on effect whereby slapdash organization eventually results in ragged on-field performances.

Interpersonal skills are perhaps the most critical category of
coaching skills since they underpin everything coaches do in
their dealings with performers, parents, officials, administrators,
sponsors, and the media. They are the vehicle for demonstrating
leadership, and include skills for motivating, teaching, con-
soling, persuading, and a host of other functions.

The relative importance of these four skill categories will
vary from sport to sport, and from individual to individual.
They may or may not all be of equal worth, but the critical
point to note is that none can be ignored or taken for granted.
No coach, no matter how knowledgeable, tactically astute and
organized, can expect to be a success without interpersonal
skills since no athlete will feel motivated to give their all for
such a coach.

Exercise 20

What is a coach?

Tick those roles you feel are involved in coaching.
Add others if appropriate.

Counsellor ☐

Trainer ☐

Organizer ☐

Motivator ☐

Disciplinarian ☐

Friend ☐

Scientist ☐

Administrator ☐

.... ☐

.... ☐

Although this chapter is concerned primarily with interpersonal skills for coaches, it is worth pursuing the overall

nature of the coaching role because your perceptions of where the boundaries of that role lie will inevitably influence your approach. Coaching demands a strange amalgam of tasks. In a well-known book on the coaching profession, 31 essential qualities and 23 distinct roles were listed, suggesting either that all coaches are very special people indeed, or that each coach constructs a personal set of functions to perform and thereby develops a unique style. Cast an eye over the list contained in **Exercise 20**. Some coaches will tick each role as an everyday part of their duties and might perhaps add a few more. Try this exercise yourself as a step towards clarifying your own coaching philosophy.

Differing Coaching Styles

In reality coaching should not be portrayed as a series of discrete functions. Inevitably they blend together into a clearly discernable style of coaching. Several coaches may perform identical functions, but because they emphasise different aspects of their role and interact with those around them in different ways they are perceived as having wildly differing styles. Brian Clough and Graham Taylor are both successful soccer coaches, and perform a similar list of coaching functions, but because of their different personalities and relationships with players have different styles.

While at least 40 distinct styles have been identified in the coaching literature, the following three basic types should be recognizable. First is the 'hard driver', an autocratic disciplinarian who preaches a doctrine of hard work, personal sacrifice and obedience to authority. Team goals are set, rules laid down and tactics decided without consulting others. Winning is the absolute priority.

Second is the 'friendly helper' who believes in democracy with views being sought before collective decisions are made. This coach encourages suggestions from athletes concerning practice and match tactics. Such a coach greatly values relationships with athletes, and may be unwilling to jeopardize them for the sake of winning.

The final kind is the 'thoughtful persuader' who ranks somewhere between the other two, being someone who manipulates rather than orders. This type of coach creates an illusion of democracy, with athletes being consulted on important issues but finally persuaded to accept the coach's views, although concessions may be made on trivial matters.

It is not possible to prescribe a definitive coaching style which will bring success in sport.

Understanding Why Athletes Compete and Coaches Coach

Everything we do is done for a reason. If an athlete loses interest in training or a coach becomes especially difficult to please, we know there is a cause, irrespective of whether it is connected with sport. Remember that the reasons for certain kinds of behaviour are rather like unshapely bodies. People do not always reveal them willingly. This reluctance may be caused by a whole range of mixed emotions, and for a coach to understand what makes an athlete tick, the coach must get to know that athlete as a person even more than as a performer. Personal insight is fundamental to squeezing the last drop of talent from an athlete.

The first recommendation for gaining an insight into an athlete involves talking to the athlete, asking questions and listening. However, it is necessary to first accept that your way of perceiving sport may not be matched by those around you. Sport has its incentives for all those involved, but the exact nature of those incentives may differ fundamentally from person to person.

A wealth of research has been conducted in Britain and America investigating the motives athletes cite for their participation in sport. The general trends outlined in **Figure 30** make interesting reading. Clearly many factors contribute to an athlete's sense of achievement, and although this list is by no means exhaustive it should provide a feel for what athletes generally seek through their involvement in sport. It is worth noting that this pattern of motives does not vary significantly between the sexes, nor across different age groups or cultures. There will of course be substantial variation from person to person, and it is this which requires the greatest sensitivity from coaches.

Very important motives
Personal improvement
Health and fitness
Making friends
Fun
Winning

Moderately important motives
Exhilaration and excitement
Feelings of personal control

Relatively unimportant motives
To intimidate or control others
Medals, trophies, etc.

Fig 30   Athletes' motives for participation in sport.

Coaches too have their own set of reasons for participation, and vary in the ways in which they judge whether they are doing a good job. The formula for successful coaching has proven as elusive as the holy grail, although in theory it should be possible to give an outline. This can be achieved by dividing coaches into the successful and unsuccessful, isolating personality or behavioural differences between them. Unfortunately this theoretical approach is undermined by the problem of clarifying exactly what we mean by a successful or unsuccessful coach. For research purposes coaches have usually been dichotomized according to whether their team wins, but this is a faulty strategy for several reasons.

Like athletes, coaches tend to have multiple reasons for their involvement in sport and hence several different criteria for judging their own success. Producing winners may not be top of the list, but either way it will almost certainly not be the sole criterion for judging themselves. Recent research involving tennis coaches has shown that in their eyes many things come above winning as indicators of success. **Figure 31** lists these indicators grouped in order of importance.

Very important indicators
Player fulfilment
Intrinsic satisfaction
Good interpersonal relationships
Development of skills
Fun for players

Moderately important indicators
Discipline and workrate of players
Coaching reputation

Relatively unimportant indicators
Winning
Money, publicity, etc.

Fig 31   Indicators of coaching success.

These indicators may not necessarily be representative of all coaches, but if they are they might be interpreted as a sign that coaches undervalue winning compared with performance. Or it might be that they are better able to keep matters in perspective. Recent debates have concerned the importance attached to winning. However, it is a curious phenomenon that winning becomes easier when less importance is attached to it. The tennis serve called out is always easier to return down the line for a winner; the relaxed state of mind induced when very little depends on the outcome of a contest often produces the best performance. Conversely, the pressure generated when winning takes on huge proportions, when everything seems to be riding on a single contest, can result in inhibited, sub-standard performances. Perhaps coaches realize that to produce winners it is necessary to deny the importance of winning, or at least to keep its importance solidly in check. Take a few minutes to consider how you assess yourself as a coach. Then complete **Exercise 21** by indicating, in order of importance, the criteria by which you judge your own success.

Interaction Theory of Coaching

A prime motive for coaching lies in the development of athletic potential, helping athletes on the journey towards athletic fulfilment. For a multiplicity of reasons, however, the translation of potential into performance, a seemingly straightforward process, often proves elusive. The simple becomes complex when three demanding forces are added to the equation (*see* **Figure 32**). Coach, athlete and situation all have their own unique, independent and often conflicting needs. None can be ignored and it is only the smooth interaction of all three which bridges the gap between potential and performance.

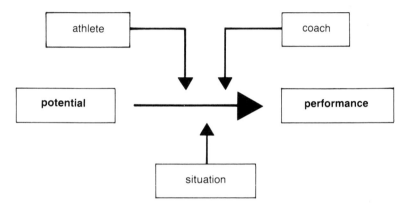

Fig 32   Forces influencing athlete performance.

Understanding exactly how these forces influence performance is not easy. A model showing how coaching style, an athlete's needs and situational demands interact to determine a result is presented in **Figure 33**. This adaptation of the leadership model by Canadian theorist, Chelladurai, suggests that a high-quality performance occurs when the coach's behavioural style (*actual* behaviour) matches that required for the particular sporting task (*prescribed* behaviour). The satisfaction of athletes, on the other hand, is dependent upon whether actual behaviour coincides with that which the athletes being coached would prefer (*preferred* behaviour).

These categories of behaviour in turn depend upon the specific characteristics of coach, athlete and situation. For example, a confident, extrovert boxing champion will prefer a different coaching style to an anxious, introverted, novice squash player. Similarly, prescribed behaviour is related to the sport being coached so, for example, the coach of a gridiron football team with perhaps 50 players all performing highly specialized and differentiated roles would need to behave very differently from the coach of a badminton team with perhaps four players all performing approximately the same role. Likewise, the model proposes that the actual behaviour of the coach tends to be determined primarily by personality and experience.

Exercise 21

How do you judge your success as a coach?

Rank the indicators you use in order of importance by placing 1, 2, 3 etc in the boxes. Add other indicators if appropriate.

Athlete fulfilment ☐

Discipline and workrate ☐

Money, publicity, etc ☐

Intrinsic satisfaction ☐

Winning performances ☐

Skill development ☐

Fun for athletes ☐

Coaching reputation ☐

Good relationships with athletes ☐

.... ☐

.... ☐

.... ☐

Ideally all three categories of behaviour should match. If there is a total mismatch between what athletes prefer, what the situation requires and what the coach actually does, then the coaching system can be chaotic. The model also proposes that outcome will have an influence upon a coach's subsequent behaviour. This infers that coaches who are sensitive to the degree of satisfaction felt by their athletes (as well as the results being produced) become flexible in their approach to coaching and do not pursue victories at the expense of their relationship with athletes. There is some research evidence that coaches of champion performers are in fact orientated even more towards the relationship with their athletes than towards winning.

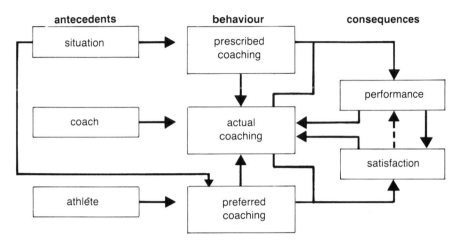

Fig 33   Interactional model of coaching.

Athlete Preferences

A coach is constantly having to decide what is best for the athletes, and to balance this with their own preferences and the demands of the situation. The trick is to ensure that the action coincides where possible with that prescribed by a task and that preferred by athletes. Good·coaches are never afraid to take unpopular decisions, but by the same token only fools are unpopular for the sake of it. Wisdom lights the way between what is necessary and what is acceptable.

A golden rule of human relationships is to be sympathetic to the idiosyncracies of the individual with whom you are dealing. However, generalizations about specific sporting groups can provide a few guiding beacons. Research into coaching preferences has usually adopted a strategy whereby different athletic groups indicate how often a coach should display a range of specific kinds of behaviour. Generalizations are made by grouping coaching behaviour, following logical and mathematical scrutiny, into categories. A common system for assessing coaches has grouped behaviour into the five categories defined in **Figure 35**. **Figure 34** shows the general pattern of athlete preferences revealed by a series of research studies. As you can see, training and instruction, and rewards, are the most eagerly

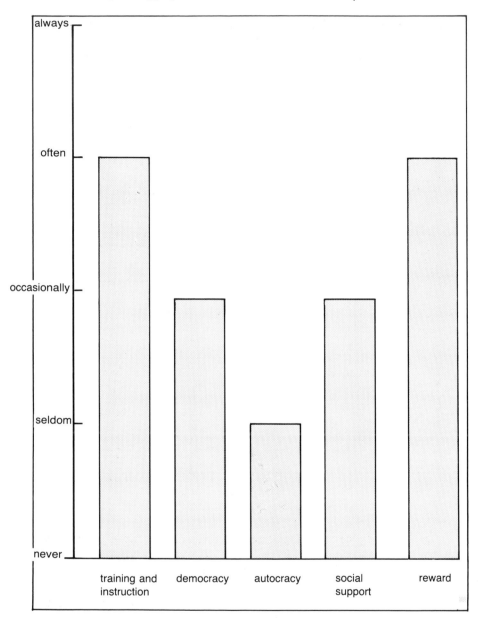

Fig 34   General pattern of athlete preferences.

sought by athletes. This suggests that, from the athlete's viewpoint, the ideal coaching environment emphasizes skill development, positive feedback, and concern for self-esteem and personal development.

Behaviour category	Description of coach's behaviour
Training and instruction behaviour	Aims at improving the performance of the athletes by emphasizing and facilitating hard and strenuous training; by instructing them in the skills, techniques and tactics of the sport; by clarifying the relationship among the members; and by structuring and co-ordinating the activities of the members.
Democratic behaviour	Allows greater participation by athletes in decisions pertaining to group goals, practice methods and game tactics and strategies.
Autocratic behaviour	Involves independent decision-making and stresses personal authority.
Social support behaviour	Characterized by a concern for individual athletes – for their welfare, for positive group atmosphere and for warm interpersonal relations with members.
Rewarding behaviour	Includes providing reinforcements for an athlete by recognizing and rewarding good performance.

Fig 35   Categories of coaching behaviour (from the work of P. Chelladurai).

A useful exercise in self-awareness is to identify your own general patterns of behaviour when coaching. Try to estimate the frequency with which you display each type of behaviour, and then compare your behavioural profile with that in **Figure 34**.

It is quite probable that whilst attempting to quantify how you behave as a coach, you raised questions regarding who you were coaching at the time; whether they were novice or expert, male or female, child or adult. The generalizations which are valid from the available research are:

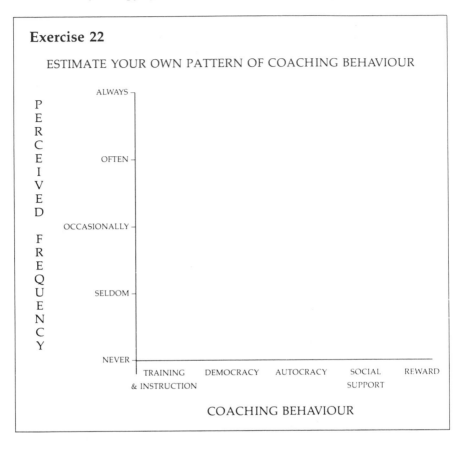

Exercise 22

ESTIMATE YOUR OWN PATTERN OF COACHING BEHAVIOUR

1.   In general, novice athletes prefer more *rewards*, and experts prefer more *democratic coaching* and *social support*.
2.   In general, team athletes prefer more *training and instruction, autocratic coaching*, and *rewards*. Individual athletes prefer more *democratic coaching* and *social support*.
3.   In general, male athletes prefer more *autocratic coaching*, and female athletes prefer more *democratic coaching*.
4.   In general, older athletes prefer more *democratic coaching, social support*, and *training and instruction*.

There is a tendency for athletes at a higher level of competition to prefer more democratic coaches, and this is particularly true in individual sports. Team athletes are sometimes prepared to sacrifice their individual preferences for the sake of group productivity, but this will vary greatly from person to person.

Male and female athletes generally tend to be much more alike than different, with varying preferences being more dependent upon the nature of the individual than gender. In contrast to a proposed stereotype, female athletes need no more social support than males, but prefer a more democratic approach. Age is a relatively unimportant variable influencing coaching preferences, although in general older, more mature athletes need more democratic coaching, more social support, and have a greater preference for training and instruction. Athletes of all ages seem to value rewards equally.

Differing Perceptions of Reality

When Robert Burns, in his ode 'To a Louse', penned the immortal line, 'O wad some Pow'r the giftie gie us, To see oursels as others see us!', he captured the challenge in all relationships. When coaches and athletes interact there is quite likely to be a discrepancy between the coach's self-perceptions and the athlete's perceptions of the coach, or vice versa. This may lead to one misinterpreting the behaviour of the other, leaving the way open for conflict brought about by misunderstanding.

To give an example, a rugby coach may encourage a young player to greater involvement in a practice match by yelling, 'C'mon son, get stuck in', a remark which the coach intends as a positive reinforcement of the efforts made so far, and a plea to raise the intensity even further. The player on the other hand may interpret this remark as a criticism of his lack of effort and perceive that the coach regards him as somehow inadequate. Never forget that the power of seemingly innocuous remarks to shape beliefs, attitudes and future behaviour is immense. Such obvious potential for misinterpretation of a coach's behaviour by players points to the general need for good communication skills among coaches.

Predicting specific areas of coaching behaviour in which perceptual discrepancies may occur is difficult, although research has revealed some discernible trends. First, there are discrepancies related to the qualitative judgements made by a coach. A classic study from the Coaching Association of Canada showed coaches tend to rate themselves as considerably more effective and knowledgeable than their athletes believe them to be. Also, coaches tend to perceive the general team climate as more ideal and less in need of change than their athletes do. Interestingly, coaches who have the best records of producing winners tend to be rated highly by their athletes, but tend to give themselves low ratings. This suggests that either humility is an important coaching attribute, or that the best coaches acknowledge how much there is still left to learn. In terms of specific behavioural categories, coaches perceive themselves to provide more training and instruction, more rewards, more social support and, perhaps surprisingly, more autocracy than athletes believe they are receiving (see **Figure 36**).

It is difficult to be precise about the reasons for these discrepancies. It may be, as already suggested, that behaviour intended by the coach to convey one message is interpreted by the player as conveying a rather different message. Alternatively, discrepancies may occur because coaches display the various categories of coaching behaviour more selectively than they realize. For instance, rewards may tend to be directed towards some players within a squad and not others. Similarly, a coach may find it possible to talk intimately only to a few performers, or may spend more time on technical instruction with certain individuals and consequently ignore others.

It is not that this selectivity should be considered wrong. In fact it is entirely consistent with the principle of catering for individual needs. However, some coaches appear to be unaware of the extent of their selectivity and concentrate too much on certain individuals and groups. It may be worth noting that research has found that the quality in a coach desired by athletes above all others is fairness. Considering what is meant by fair, one could conclude that all athletes have a right of equal access to your time and experience.

Bearing in mind this evidence, spend a few minutes reviewing your estimate of how you coach from **Exercise 22**. It could be inferred that coaches see themselves the way they think they are, whereas athletes see them the way they really are. Research in this area also shows that where the discrepancy between the coach's self perceptions and the athlete's perceptions of the coach is large the athlete tends to be dissatisfied with the coach, which in time may cause a serious decline in results. The moral is the need for coach and athlete alike to view what the coach does 'through a single eye', as it were. This level of mutual understanding will only develop if clear channels of communication are established which allow individuals the opportunity to express their own views, needs, hopes and fears. It would therefore appear that talking and listening are at the heart of effective coaching.

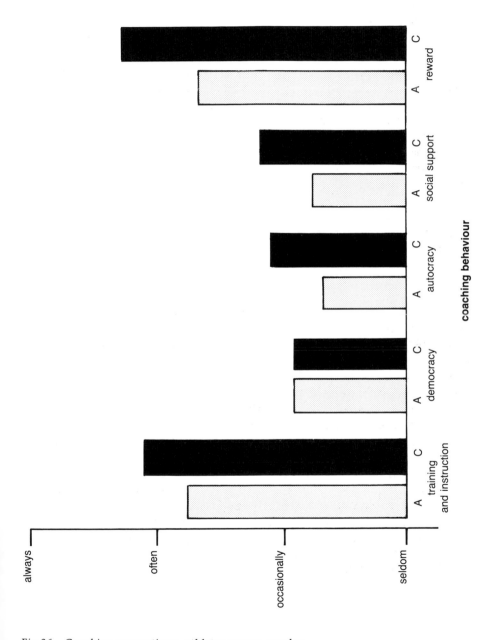

Fig 36   Coaching perceptions: athletes versus coaches.

Recommendations for Effective Coaching

In making recommendations it is proposed that key aspects of coaching skills are the ability to motivate, the need for effective communication, and the demonstration of leadership qualities.

Motivation

In coaching, motivation seeks to improve an athlete's commitment and results, maintaining persistance towards personal goals, and enhancing the overall experience of the sport and so guaranteeing continued involvement. Any attempt which a coach makes to motivate performers should be judged against these criteria. The list of motivation techniques proposed in many excellent books on the subject is long, but it is possible to translate the principles of motivation into some straightforward recommendations.

1.   Personality has a major impact upon motivation levels, therefore get to know and understand athletes as individuals.
2.   Motivation is boosted by variety, therefore introduce new and stimulating training activities periodically or occasionally transfer practice sessions to a fresh environment.
3.   Encourage athletes to recognize the link between levels of effort and performance. It is very important for motivation that the route to success is perceived by athletes as being within their control.
4.   If competition is used to motivate groups of performers, use it in a form where every person believes they have a chance of winning.
5.   Goal setting is frequently proposed as an effective motivation device, but done badly it probably has the opposite effect. Set goals which enhance an athlete's feelings of competence and personal control.
6.   Athletes like to be rewarded for their efforts and will work hard for even a scrap of praise from the coach. The overriding principle of any reward structure is that it must be perceived as consistent and fair by all concerned.
7.   Role models can provide inspiration to young performers. Pictures or quotes from successful performers which emphasize that the road to glory starts from humble beginnings and is soaked with sweat help to maintain consistent effort.

Communication

The first lesson of effective communication is to realize that there will usually be a discrepancy between what the sender of a message intends, and what the receiver understands by it. Every word or gesture is open to misinterpretation and therefore developing communication skills is fundamental to coaching. Unfortunately, bad listening habits such as failing to concentrate on what is being said to you, or showing a lack of interest, or interrupting, or hogging the speaking role are all too common. Some fundamental 'rules' of communication are:

1.   Be a good listener.
2.   When speaking, accept responsibility for communicating clearly.
3.   Seek clarification that your message has been received and understood.
4.   Use simple, direct language.
5.   Be aware that body language communicates as powerfully as words.

Leadership

No one knows the universal formula for effective leadership. Learning to exert influence occurs gradually, but gaining respect and winning the hearts of those you lead may occur more readily if certain general suggestions are followed.

1.   Sincerity, commitment to personal beliefs, and individuality are linked to effective leadership, therefore be yourself.
2.   Consistency of approach is important, therefore be clear about the style which suits you, your situation and those you hope to influence.
3.   Creating a favourable environment is critical, therefore clarify objectives, expectations and procedures after consultation with others. Don't be afraid to delegate some degree of authority, provide regular feedback for those you are leading, and show consideration for their individual needs.
4.   Recognize that getting the coaching job done is achieved through the efforts of other people, and therefore sensitivity to the needs of athletes is the way to inspire commitment and loyalty from them.
5.   Do not fear self-evaluation and be prepared to change. Flexibility in your approach is not a weakness.

A theme throughout this chapter has been that life holds no simple answers. Relationships are complicated and ultimately only you can find the path of success. Experience continues to be the best teacher, but awareness of the research findings outlined here may speed your progress. It appears that in sport the losers have all the answers, while the winners ask all the questions. Hopefully, you will have asked a few questions of yourself and, in doing so, progressed a few paces further towards your personal ambitions.

CHAPTER EIGHT

Team Building: The Development of Team Spirit

John Syer

Defined technically, team spirit occurs in two ways – as synergy and as confluence. In the first case it is the creative energy expressed by a group of individuals whose strength and ability as a unit is greater than the sum of that possessed by them individually. In the second, it is the sense of belonging experienced by each member of such a team.

A team that has team spirit provides the individual member with two big assets; an additional source of resolve in times of stress and clear feedback on personal performance. These are commodities of such obvious value to coaches that, even when coaching individual sports, they will automatically treat squad members as a team.

In those sports where a squad is unusual – such as tennis and golf – top players form a back-up team around them. Most athletes know that they cannot develop, improve or change until they are fully aware of what they are doing. This awareness can only come from feedback. Nick Faldo still needs David Leadbetter.

Since athletic performance has physical, technical, emotional and mental components, a whole spectrum of honest feedback is required. As this is normally supplied by a coach and other team members the quality of an athlete's relationships and the communication within the team directly affects performance. Honest feedback is only given when team members experience trust, respect and team spirit.

All athletes, whatever their sport, can improve team spirit and thereby their own performance by opening or strengthening personal lines of communication with the people around them. However, in team sports, the athletes' attempt to team-build are either stunted or reinforced by the captain or coach. Consequently, you can probably build team spirit instinctively by your own style of communication, and by your natural ability to help your team members to communicate openly with each other. The essential point is that *programmed* team mental training can speed this process.

As with individual mental training, you would probably benefit from the assistance of a good sport psychologist since initially some of the skills and many of the exercises required will be foreign to you. Yet, whereas individual mental training demands time which you will not often have (in addition to specific skills), much of team mental training is done at the team meetings when you are in charge. Either way, your attitude and approach will always affect team spirit. So let's explore team mental training or team-building in relation to your role.
Team building may be defined as:

1.   A part of every team leader's job:
2.   An awareness of the needs and ambitions of individual members.
3.   A way of relating to team members.
4.   Helping team members to understand each other better.
5.   An awareness of the potential of the team as a unit.
6.   An attitude.
7.   A way of conducting meetings.
8.   Conducting exercises that promote communication.

The rest of this chapter examines each of these factors in turn.

Team Building by the Team Leader

Many managers in industry equate team building with outward-bound courses, and send their teams away to tramp over mountain and bog in winter or the depth of the night. Very often the team returns in high good humour and enough funny stories to last a month. The manager also feels good. Having opted out at the last moment, due to sudden imperative demands from higher up the ladder, the manager not only dealt with the emergency but was able to get rid of some backlog of work as well. Assured that all went well and having listened patiently to some of the team's anecdotes, the manager is inclined to send more staff on a similar venture.

Such experiences can be valuable but, under such circumstances, once the team members are back in their office the experience will soon be forgotten and the old patterns of relationship re-established. A manager who wants lasting results must follow the example of Doug Beale, America's men's volleyball coach, who brought his team from 15th in the world to a gold medal at the 1984 Olympics. Doug involved his players in a similar experience but did two things differently. First, he was personally involved throughout, from initial planning to final review and second on their return, he made review the key part of the process.

Only participation and 'processing' ensure success. Processing is the review of an experience by the participants, facilitated by the coach or team leader, with everyone having a chance to say what they noticed or discovered, what they imagined and what they felt. Without processing, your athletes will never learn that their experience of the same event can be different, and that each has a personal set of values and needs which may be different from those of everyone else. Without processing nothing is made of the experience and, even though certain individuals may gain some insight, the team itself does not gain and grow.

Any unusual experience will provide your team members with new insights into each other, highlighting strengths and weaknesses that had not been fully apparent before. It can also provide a reference point for team spirit, adding words and new concepts to your team's own idiom. This is the experience of the club team on its first tour. Yet your team will learn little of importance unless it is processed at a team meeting, and in meetings between small groups or pairs of athletes with yourself. In fact, no team gets maximum profit from any training session or match without some degree of processing. This means stopping occasionally to prompt your athletes to explore, express and debate their personal experience of the event, instead of laying down the law.

Individual mental training requires athletes to think about their personal performance in various, specific ways. Team building or team mental training asks them to communicate their observations, ideas and feelings to each other. If you do not establish a norm of two-way communication between yourself and your team members, and do not foster similar two-way communication between your team members, you are not team building and will not develop team spirit. No one else in the team can do the job for you. If a team has no leader, or if the leader's role is not made clear, the group as a whole will probably operate *less* effectively than the sum of its parts.

Team Building and Individual Needs

Team building, like parenting, requires a combination of caring and detachment. It also demands clarity with regards to your own motivation. Otherwise, as in all positions of responsibility, there is the danger that you will unconsciously use athletes to your own ends. If you care, are aware of and honest about your own ambitions and can take a detached view of the whole, you will discover more and more about the different needs and ambitions of each of your team members.

Watching carefully requires that you do not always hold centre stage. This is easy enough during training and competition but may not be the norm at team meetings. If you have inherited a team where the previous coach was long on talk and short on listening, you may find that such behaviour disconcerts your athletes and that, reluctant to show their observations and opinions, they fall back on clowning around. If so, ask a question and ask them each to write down their answer. As they write you can watch.

You are already no longer centre stage and silence changes the prevailing atmosphere. After a moment either split them into groups of three to discuss what they have written, or ask each in turn to read out their answer and then discuss their different ideas together. Either way, the focus remains on them.

Once you have established such a vantage point, one that your team can accept, retreat to it periodically to see what is happening. As coach you need to acquire the ability to see and hear without jumping to immediate conclusions. When the time comes to return centre stage (as of course you must), state what you have noticed, add if you wish what you imagine and ask for your athletes' response. If what you notice provokes some strong emotion, you can add what you feel – 'I'm excited . . . I'm furious . . . I'm relieved . . . I'm bitterly disappointed' – but hold back from judgements and opinions until you have had their response. (Notice that any sentence that begins with 'I feel that . . .' constitutes an opinion, not a feeling.)

This objective style – describing what you see, what you hear and perhaps what you imagine and what you feel – is an essential component of team-building. It removes threat, creates trust, shows respect and promotes openness. As you begin to model the style make it explicit and help your team to adopt it themselves as they speak to each other, especially during feedback sessions at training or after a competitive event. Spell it out. Ask them 'to say what you have noticed, say what you imagine (and check it out), say how you feel, and *then* offer whatever suggestion you may have.'

Any discussion conducted along these lines will reflect the different needs and ambitions of each individual, and give clues as to how they can be merged into the objectives of the whole team. That said, team meetings are not enough. Not only need you be available to each athlete on a one-to-one basis, but you should actively seek each of them out, preferably in their own surroundings, and allow them to explain the context of their involvement with the team, the wider perspective.

As coach to the Scottish men's volleyball team, I visited most of the players at home, at work, or at their places of study. I would chat with them in pubs, on the telephone, in cars and in trains. John Madden, one of the greatest American football coaches, used to go to the locker room and speak to each player at least once each day. Alan Jones, the Australian rugby coach, would telephone each of his players once a week from Europe, whenever he was on a seminar or coaching tour. This requires planning and more time than you think you may have, but it becomes a priority in the context of building team spirit and helping the team to achieve its potential.

How many athletes are there in your team – seven? That is the number of relationships you must foster. Which of these relationships are the strongest? Which the weakest? Your team is no stronger than the weakest of these links.

What will you do in the next three days to strengthen one of these relationships? I recently asked this question to the coach of one of the national teams I work with and he replied: 'Get to know Paul better.' This was not good enough: 'How are you going to do that?' I asked. 'Spend time with him', came the reply. 'When are you going to do that?' I asked. 'I'll have to phone him', the coach answered. 'And when will you phone?' 'You want me to say now? OK, I'll phone tomorrow morning and arrange a meeting for later this week.' (And he did.)

Team Building is a Way of Relating to Team Members.

As a coach, inadequate as I sometimes felt, I became aware that I was working in the field of education. I told my players what I knew, I explained my ideas, I said what I wanted but none of that seemed to get very far unless I asked them to report an experience. 'What did you notice?' 'What did you discover?' 'How did you feel?' 'What were you aware of doing?' 'How did you do that?' are questions which lead athletes to consult their own feelings – both kinaesthetic and emotional. On the other hand, 'Why on earth did you do that?' invites justification or opinions. Instead of 'Why?', ask 'What?', 'How?' 'Where?, and 'When?'. Instead of giving answers based on your own knowledge or assumptions, start with questions. If the athlete cannot

'Synergy' is the creative energy expressed by a group of individuals when ability as a unit is greater than the sum of that possessed by them individually.

answer, then repeat the routine asking that he or she focuses their attention more specifically on what they do at a certain moment. If that does not work, record them on video and show the result. Only when athletes know what they are doing are they able to improve and change. This applies to mental and emotional patterns of behaviour as well as to physical and technical patterns. Helping your team members to become aware of what they do, before judging what they do, allows them to discover a more effective, efficient and therefore correct mode of performance.

Motivation is inherent in such discoveries, especially once the members of your team have expressed their ambitions and helped formulate the vision of the team as a whole. Team building involves helping each individual to take responsibility for their own experience. Motivation can be inspired by example, but has to be fostered and fuelled from within.

Encourage the expression of different points of view without taking a polarized position *vis-à-vis* any of your team members. Agree to differ, come to a decision but do not deny anyone's experience. Rather, help the athlete concerned to explore and report on that experience further. Show that you value the resistance and believe there might be some factor at the root of it which is of benefit to the team as a whole. Above all, notice that the athlete who seems to oppose you can at least be appreciated for being alert, committed to the issue and fully engaged.

As your skills develop you will welcome conflict as a potentially creative process. The wealth of differences in outlook, as well as skill that exists in your team, would be wasted if you did not allow and encourage the expression of conflicting opinions. Only then is there the possiblity of the team discovering an idea that no individual could have produced alone. This is a practical product of synergy that is available to any committed group of people as they become a genuine team.

Team Building and Helping Individuals to Understand Each Other

Only an awareness of yourself – your own ambitions, needs and patterns of behaviour – allows an awareness of others and of how they are different. Only when you appreciate these differences can you make real contact and communicate properly with the members of your team. Yet, having gained an awareness of yourself and an appreciation of how you are different, having established contact, respect and trust between yourself and each member of your team, you still need to create a climate where the same process may occur between each pair of athletes if you are to help team spirit to evolve.

You can do this through a combination of descriptive feedback and a variety of team building exercises. As a starting point, help your athletes to discover that it is only when they know when and how to pay attention to their individual needs that they will be able to appreciate who they are with, and contribute fully to the team. Athletes who are unable to withdraw from the team in this way, rarely live up to their potential, frequently misunderstand their team mates and are often the first to get injured. Establish clearly the right and necessity for individuals to spend time alone or quietly, and discuss the timing of this. You can discuss self-assessment and individual training programmes – physical, technical and mental – in this context.

Team Building is an Awareness of the Potential of the Team as a Unit

Whilst team building demands that you give your full attention to each team member and to specific relationships within the team, you have to retain the ability to pull back and tune in to the potential of the team as a whole. What is the pattern that allows each individual to contribute fully to the whole? Viewed this way, what is the nature and identity of the team? Each member will tune in to this supreme identity from time to time, be inspired by it, and have a strong sense of belonging. Team identity and team vision will be closely allied. As team leader and team-builder you will 'hold' this vision at times when others forget.

Of course, it takes time to become fully aware of your team's potential. As each member develops, the true identity of the team becomes clearer. When a member leaves or a new member joins the kaleidoscope is shaken and the picture will change. Yet a pattern does emerge. As you become aware of each individual you begin to experience the team as being greater than the sum of its parts. Team building is then a matter of helping each member to experience and tune in to this feeling at will.

Since such an experience is the result of hard work, over a considerable period of time, it will be reflected in a wide variety of routines, catchwords, and norms. Used correctly any of these has the power to focus simultaneously each individual's attention on the team's vision and prime objective. As team leader and team-builder your detachment allows you to know when and how to use such touchstones and gradually to pass on this awareness to the rest of your team.

Team Building is an Attitude.

This is the simplest definition of all, and one from which other definitions are derived. If you can recognize what it is that you would like the team to become but realize that such a preconceived idea will be limiting, your attitude becomes one of discovery. Reflect on all that you know about each individual and then sit back and ask 'How could this be? What is the perfect pattern within which the potential of each individual is fulfilled?'

Holding an image in your mind and heart of the best performance and expression of each team member, and the best of the team as a whole is also team building. Your first attempts to tune in to such an image you may fail, but gradually something will emerge which you will then see with increasing clarity. As team leader you are guardian of this image and should refer to it constantly.

This is not easy. The temptation to express your frustration to outsiders or to be critical about certain team members can be strong, and each time you do this the image of the team's potential will diminish. If one individual has a series of below par performances you may unthinkingly begin to be critical and say 'Bill always cracks under pressure' or 'Joan's concentration is zero', whilst not speaking in such terms to the athlete concerned. The manager of one football club that Christopher Connolly, my consultancy partner, and I both worked with did not have one good word to say about a particular player. One afternoon in his office I mentioned this player's name. Before I'd finished talking, the manager broke in to say 'He's *always* getting booked: he's a real liability, however classy his skills might be.' I looked up at the board behind him where every player and every booking of the season was listed. It was April – one more month of the season to go – and there in black and white was the information that the player had only been booked once all season. When I pointed this out the manager looked surprised and said 'Oh, it must have been last year's performance I was remembering.'

We knew this player was becoming isolated from the rest of the team. A lesser or younger player would have felt trapped and ultimately crushed by such hostility. There was no point suggesting that the manager be more meticulous in his assessment, but we did ask him to say three things that he appreciated about the player and to write these down.

Affirming the best in a team member or holding an image of the team's potential becomes easier with practice. Sit back for a moment and complete **Exercise 23**.

Exercise 23

Take a deep breath, hold it a moment and then
slowly exhale. Next, think of each of your athletes
in turn, visualizing a specific moment when each
did something perfect, perhaps after a long series of
failed attempts. Remember one positive interchange
that you have had with each athlete and, if that is difficult, visualize a time when that athlete interacted
positively with another member of the team. Then
recall a moment when your team did something
perfectly as a unit, either in competition or while
training. 'Play' that memory through, remembering
how you felt.

As a coach you have only a limited degree of influence over
what your athletes actually do, but you can gain complete
control over your response to their actions and over your basic
attitude towards them. Each of these positive memories can be a
touchstone for you in affirming the best. Each time you practise
such visualizations you will align yourself more strongly with
the team's potential, and in so doing will become more of an
inspiration to the team itself.

Team Building is a Way of Conducting Meetings

One of the most valued skills of a business manager is the ability
to lead effective meetings. This may seem less important for a
coach, but in fact it is a key aspect of team building, especially
if meetings are defined as any encounter between the coach and
team member or members. Meetings are most easily classified
according to size: one-to-one, pairs, small groups and full team.
There are variations within each category.

ONE-TO-ONE MEETINGS

This involves spending time with one team member. The meetings may happen in your room or office, their home, alone in the
locker room, out on a walk or in a restaurant, and they will always
have some stated or unstated purpose.

There is the initial welcoming meeting (or with a professional
team an interview) at which the athlete tells you about his or
her past experience and current goals, and you explain the
team set-up – the rules and the season's objectives. You also

explain the role you have in mind for this athlete and what you want the athlete to concentrate on during the first few days. This category of 'initial' one-to-one meetings includes the time you spend with each athlete in turn at the start of the season, mid-season, at the start of a new initiative, or at the start of your own tenure of office, where you see each team member in turn.

The other two kinds of one-to-one meetings are feedback meetings and 'counselling' discussions. The first concerns the individual's performance and its relationship to the team's objectives and tactics. The athlete is asked to assess his or her performance in terms of physical, technical and mental skills. You then give your views and discuss new personal goals, ending with a personal training programme that ideally includes mental as well as physical and technical exercises.

'Counselling' meetings are rare and more discursive. Athletes should not feel obliged to recount details of their life away from the team but, as coach, you will find occasions where this may happen. In chatting to your athletes about work, study, vacation and family you have the opportunity to show another side of yourself and model both trust and respect. Such availability and two-way communication may be an understated but important balance to the demands for intense effort that are part and parcel of your normal training session. Also, this availability will model and mirror the availability of the team as a whole for any of its members. A synergistic team – a team with team spirit – is a source of support, vitality and strength for each of its members.

PAIRS MEETINGS

If you are coach to a squad or team of 12 individuals, there will be 66 different paired units within that team, plus another 12 if you include each individual's relationship with you. Each pairing within the team holds the potential for additional insight and team spirit; each pairing has a different character, identity and strength – not just different from each other but also from each individual within the team. Usually these pairings are an untapped resource.

Pairs meetings consist of a leader and two members. We identify two types of pairs meeting: tactical meetings and 'constructed' conversations. In tactical meetings the leader will invariably be yourself. Here you review the way that two athletes perform in relation to each other during competition. You ask for their own descriptive feedback – what each noticed, what they imagine, and what they feel – and then give your own views. Afterwards you invite suggestions, give your suggestions and come to a new set of objectives. You then hammer out a training programme for them as a unit.

This is something which you are sure to be doing instinctively, if informally, with certain pairings – although you may only think of such meetings when something has gone wrong. Each possible pairing should meet to discuss how they see their separate performances affecting each other, and how they might make this connection work more smoothly. However, with a team larger than four you would have to delegate the exercise either to the players themselves or to members of your coaching staff, given the demands such a project would place on your time.

I devised the second type of pairs meeting – constructed conversations – during the years I worked with Tottenham Hotspur Football Club, and have continued to develop it with both sport and business teams ever since. It is now a key part of our team building work.

This is not the place to expand on it in detail, since it is an exercise which you would initially need some help in leading. Suffice to say that it is based on sentence completion and can have a considerable impact, even with team members who have competed together for years and get on with each other well. It allows things to be said which an athlete has hesitated to say before. It improves understanding and enhances awareness. It is clearly useful for two athletes who interact tactically, especially if one has been in the team longer than the other. The new athlete may have brought a tactical sense based on the patterns of a previous team and not have realized the fine adjustments that need to be made. For two athletes who avoid each other, dislike each other, lack respect or simply do not take opportunities to speak to each other, such an exercise is particularly appropriate.

SMALL TEAM MEETINGS
Most teams of more than ten members break down into smaller technical or tactical groups. Each can also become a source of team spirit, having its own role, objectives and action plan which contributes to the whole. An American professional football team is so large that each tactical grouping has its own set of coaches. In this case the leading coach of each group forms another 'small team' with the club's head coach as their own leader. Indeed, in most national and professional teams the coaching staff form a distinct small team of their own.

The level of team spirit within each group directly affects

the whole. This is especially true of the coaching staff. One foreign national team I had just begun working with a few years ago had a coaching staff that divided into two camps. Things were so bad that a tremendous argument broke out in a hotel lobby shortly after the team arrived at a major tournament. The athletes' morale dropped visibly and the next morning training was abysmal. I suggested a nightly coaching staff meeting. This was conducted along the lines we had established earlier with the athletes – paying some attention to how we were each feeling, before reviewing the day. Within 24 hours the climate within the team as a whole had completely changed.

Teams tend to divide tactically. Volleyball teams have setters, outside hitters, middle blockers. Soccer teams have full backs (plus goalkeeper), midfield and strikers. Cricket teams have players who bowl and players who bat, with those who bat dividing into openers and middle-order, and bowlers dividing into fast, medium and spin. Each group has its own view of the team's performance and it is well worth while to create time within the team meeting to break into these groups. This gives each group the opportunity to discuss its view of a given topic, and to decide both what it is they need from the other groups and what they have to offer.

We first did this at Tottenham when staying overnight at hotels prior to the FA Cup matches in 1981–82. Initially Keith Burkinshaw, the manager, wanted to sit in on the discussions but it became obvious that the group he chose to sit with was always the quietest and that when left alone, having been given a particular task or topic, the group discussions were far livelier.

With some teams I have worked with, the coach or manager has had reservations about dividing the team into small groups. 'What if they just argue with each other? It could be divisive.' The answer to this is that, yes, in a team that lacks team spirit, that has not gained a sense of identity and has not been given the chance to express views openly, there may be cliques beneath the surface that are barely visible. Discussion would uncover these divisions but would also allow the different sides to understand better and learn from each other. If there are no such divisions already, breaking into small groups is not going to create them, although it may create differing opinions, quite hotly held, which hold the potential for new insight. If the divisions are there, though hidden, they will have a strongly adverse effect on the team's performance.

If you wish to experiment with this team building technique, use **Exercise 24**.

Exercise 24

Decide on your small groupings before the meeting,
and the topic that you want your athletes to discuss.
Write the topic clearly on a flip chart and give them
a set amount of time to talk. Five minutes before that
time is up, ask them to agree on a summary and to
elect a spokesperson, and then involve everyone in
the feedback, further discussion, and decisions.

FULL TEAM MEETINGS

Full team meetings can be divided into talks, discussions and
celebrations. With an amateur team, celebrations can be a weekly
event. The Edinburgh University men's volleyball team, where I
learned as much about team spirit as in any psychology class,
would celebrate win or lose – often with our opponents and
always with food, drink and music – after every home match.
Keith Burkinshaw, an astute but retiring manager, was astonished
at the appreciation he unleashed by inviting the team back to his
office on returning from one particularly important away win.
(The celebrations on our return from Wembley with the FA Cup
in 1981 and 1982 were more predictable.)

It was with Keith too that we had to distinguish between
talk and discussions. When we first arrived he was holding
his Monday morning post-match review meeting, standing with
his coach Peter Shreeve behind a table and facing the players
who sat in a row in front of him. He began with a question but
immediately answered it himself. He then asked for comments
('Come on, this is a discussion, isn't it?') and got none. The next
Saturday, at Aston Villa, he walked into the locker room as the
players were changing. 'OK, do you all know what we're doing?'
he asked and turned as someone behind him said 'What about
penalties, Keith?', and then turned again as someone else replied
'You know about penalties, we practised them on Tuesday', and
turned *again* as a third player said 'He wasn't there on Tuesday'
. . . and so it continued. Keith had intended a pre-match talk and
had found himself embroiled in a discussion.

The answer was easy enough. From then on, Monday morning
meetings were held with everyone sitting in a circle of chairs.
Keith would ask a question and invite the younger players to
answer first. Because they were sitting in a circle, he was able
to deflect any questions made directly to him and encourage
his players to answer each other. He got a discussion and for

the first time outside the locker room, the players became really engaged. (The same happened at Queens Park Rangers when I worked there with Jim Smith, some six or seven years later.) On match days, the players were asked to stop changing and move to one side of the room. Keith stood up and, instead of asking a question, reminded the team briefly of the tactics that had been agreed upon earlier in the week. There was no come-back: this was a team talk.

Remember that while you may give a talk to impart information, prematch talks are primarily to evoke team spirit. Discussion meetings are designed to build it. When team building, these are the meetings which concern us most.

Pause for a moment and complete **Exercise 25**.

Exercise 25

Consider how you hold team meetings. Do you permit discussion at appropriate times? Consider any changes you could make to facilitate more productive team meetings, and more efficient team talks.

Task, Maintenance and Process

Successful discussion meetings – whether one-to-one, pairs, small group or full team – have three components: task, maintenance and process. Task is the topic, agenda or business of the meeting – a discussion of past performance, of an opponent's style, or of tactics for the next competition. This is the main part of any discussion meeting and is the place for ideas, suggestions, opinions, objections, argument and decisions. Maintenance is time spent attending to how people feel. Good meetings begin with a period of maintenance that may be termed warming up. At this stage, one pays attention to all factors – the place where the meeting is held and the arrangement of the furniture, the frame of mind and state of body in which one arrived, the other individuals present and the character of the team as a unit – that may affect feelings and thereby performance. Maintenance is introduced mid-way through the meeting, by stopping to ask how people are feeling, taking a coffee break, telling a joke, opening a window, having a stretch – anything that attends to what people need in the moment. Maintenance also includes warming down, checking how people feel before the meeting ends and tuning in once more to the identity of the team. Warming up and warming down are an essential part of team building because they are a time for individuals to recognize their own needs, to become fully aware of each other and to tune in to the identity of the team as a whole. By paying attention to the place where you meet – arranging the room to suit your purpose or, for an impromptu review in a crowded tournament sportshall, creating a space of your own to help focus attention – you are then free to address the purpose of the meeting and the format or agenda.

The third component of a meeting, process, is required whenever the meeting has gone off course. It involves stepping back for a moment and taking a look at the dynamic of the meeting. Processing only occurs in the middle of a meeting (maintenance is required at the beginning and at the end as well). Maintenance is a break from task, processing is a break from task or maintenance. When you feel a need for maintenance, you might say 'How about taking a break?' or 'Let's see how everyone's feeling.' When you feel a need for process, you will say 'OK, so what do we notice? What's happening here?'

The response to a shift to maintenance might be 'Yes, I'm shattered, let's come back in five minutes' or I'm really frustrated with Joe; Joe you never give an inch!' The response to your proposed shift to process would be 'I notice that Joe and Peter have been arguing for five minutes and that nobody else has said anything. I notice that Jeff had doodled patterns over half of a sheet of paper. I notice that Dave is looking out of the window and that you have been talking quietly to Edward whilst Joe and Peter argue.'

Processing is a buffer to keep the meeting on the rails. As a result you may decide to get back to the agenda, ask for other ideas or opinions, or you may want to move into maintenance and ask how people are feeling: either 'OK, Joe, why don't you check out what someone else thinks of your idea?' (going back to task), or 'Dave, how do you feel when Joe and Peter go on like this?' (changing for a moment to maintenance). Process regulates the time spent on task and maintenance. (Normally task takes up 80 per cent of a good meeting.)

If there is too much task, suppressed feelings will block progress. If there is too much maintenance (checking out how people feel), nothing gets decided. The most common fault of those who lead meetings (after not allowing discussion at all) is leaving no time for maintenance or process. The result is a team which has secret cliques and a short attention span.

Leading a Full Team Meeting

1.   *Asking v. telling.* Most discussions need a preamble to set the scene – a set of choices, factual information – but if you start by giving your own opinion the younger and less experienced athletes may never get involved. Others who disagree with you may not like to say so, and those who do disagree risk being labelled trouble-makers. Any real discussion tends to disintegrate into a series of dialogues between you and other individuals in turn. Creativity founders. After your preamble, show the flip chart with the topic or question, ask them to write a response and then divide them into threes so that even the quietest get an opportunity to talk before returning to a full team discussion.

2.   *Watching v. talking.* If you have no assistant it is doubly important to turn attention away from yourself so that you can concentrate on individual patterns of behaviour, patterns of reaction, and of interaction.

3.   *Seeing individuals v. seeing the team.* Many coaches only consider their team as a unit, and speak to them as a unit. This will avoid important information available from individual players, and an opportunity to see beyond present performance towards the team's potential. As you scan the circle of athletes, notice the assumptions you make and your reactions to what you see and hear. Note them down and throw in a question or two to keep the pot boiling and the discussion focused on the chosen topic. Then occasionally consider the whole. Ask yourself the process questions 'What's going on here? What's the big picture?' and see what comes to mind. Then call for a process check and see what they notice.

4.   *Diverting attention v. demanding attention.* The best time for you to talk is at the beginning (to introduce the topic) and the end. If athletes appeal to you, as certain athletes always will, give information but withhold opinions until it is time to conclude. If necessary, counter questions with another question that directs the team's attention to something they may be missing. During competition they must find their own answers, and for this too they should train. Paradoxically, the less you demand attention the better your athletes will hear what you have to say when you speak: diverting attention does not divest you of influence. Demand attention too often and your athletes will switch off.

Principles for all Participants

These are team building principles of discussion. Perhaps you already follow them; if not, give them a try and notice the results. Then, as you refine and make them explicit, they will become norms for your team. Eventually the athletes themselves will coach new members and ensure continuity.

1.   *Descriptive feedback.* In discussing performance, say what you noticed and, if necessary, what you imagine and what you feel. Most judgements and opinions are based on what you imagine, as are your feelings. Make this explicit. Later you can offer suggestions.

2.   *Speak to, not about.* Listen carefully and you will notice that the athletes who appeal most often to your judgement also tend to talk about other team members who are sitting there listening. Each time this happens – each time someone says 'Joe gets it right' or 'Joe gets it wrong' – redirect their attention by saying 'Tell *him*', even when they are fully involved in their story. If they do not get it, be explicit: 'Look at Joe, use his name and say "you" not "he" – talk *to* him, not about him. He's here.' Each time they get it, the effect is electric: real contact is made, to the surprise of both athletes. At Queens Park Rangers this was the principle which manager Jim Smith latched on to first. After four team meetings he reported: 'All of you are communicating better and offering your observations . . . [you're] more aware of your team-mates' duties and your own duties and how you can help yourselves be more positive and confident on the pitch . . . there's a better feeling amongst everybody and that's also very important.'

3.   *Give personal response.* Whilst deflecting appeals to your judgement until most others have had their say, allow the team to see that you are fully involved. You are part of it, even though you have a special role. Allow them to know what's happening to you from time to time, as the discussion continues. Modelling availability is important, since some athletes will not find it easy to participate. Point out that each time someone speaks, especially if it is to give a personal response, it is a gift to other members of the team. As George Brown, Professor of Confluent Education at the University of California at Santa Barbara, says: 'Such a gift is like those we get at Christmas – sometimes it's something we can use immediately, sometimes it's something we put away in a drawer in case we can use it later, and sometimes it's something we know we can't use and put in the trash can.'

4.   *Feelings can't be wrong, feelings aren't logical.* The distinction

between saying what you think and saying what you feel is crucial. When athletes say what they think, they are expressing an opinion and can be argued with. When athletes say what they feel no-one can argue and, more often than not, they are giving useful information to the team.

Team Building is Conducting Exercises that Promote Communication

In devising an experiential five-day team building course for team managers at Ford Motor Company, my colleague and I recently discovered that we'd invented over 200 team building exercises, each with many variations, in the space of 10 years. Most of them had been devised in the previous three years, as our prime focus shifted from individual to team mental training.

There is not the space in this chapter to go into this much detail, but underlying all exercises are certain principles, and the best exercises will be those that you devise for a particular situation that has arisen in the team. Here are some of the things to consider as you decide what to do.

1. *Ensure groupings are either selected or random.* Athletes, like members of any group or team, tend to sit next to people they know or like best. Either form groupings that ensure members each meet someone you want them to meet, or create groups ensuring that groupings are random.
2. *Everyone meet everyone.* Keep changing the groupings (which is more important than changing the topic). In fact, to keep the same topic and encourage discussion with as many members as possible, helps each member to appreciate, learn from and respect differences.
3. *Make issues explicit.* If you listen to your athletes talking, you will discover from week to week that issues will surface. Listen for key words and devise your exercises around them. We've done this with honesty, with trust, with confidence, with change, with substitution, with character and many other words. Think of exercises which will give your team a direct experience of the issue, so that you have a two-fold basis for discussion afterwards: (i) the experience of the exercise, and (ii) the issue as it is experienced within the team.
4. *Remember the sequence.* Team mental training exercises will be as surprising to your team as individual mental training exercises, so proceed in easy steps. The simplest exercises are those which involve athletes writing down their thoughts and then discussing

what they have written. Start always by asking players to 'tune in' to themselves: self-awareness precedes the ability to be fully aware of others, and to appreciate how others are different. Then let them take the second step, meeting one person at a time. Contact, communication and a greater depth of understanding will follow. Eventually respect and trust appear and deeper concerns and feelings are expressed. Each exercise can build on the previous one.

5.   *Vary the type of exercise.* Some exercises are done sitting down, some standing up, some with the athletes moving around and mingling. Simple exercises exchange opinions and ideas, others are without words. There are exercises with drawing, with music, with acting. Some exercises involve physical contact, some need as much space as possible, some are competitive, some co-operative, and some done in isolation. Everything in the room may be used for something other than its prime purpose. Some exercises are children's games, some are complicated puzzles. Be clear about the lesson you want the exercise to illustrate, and then see how many ways you can think of to bring the lesson home.

6.   *Always leave time for feedback.* Any team experience offers insight to the team's potential. Each member of the team sees one part of the truth. Discussion of the experience – be it a competition, a training session or a mental training exercise – provides the opportunity for a few more parts of the puzzle to be put in place. Team building exercises usually leave athletes feeling good, but if the feeling is not tied down to some shared understanding of the message involved in the exercise, nothing much is left when the feeling fades. Make sure there is always time for feedback.

When team building is established as part of the training routine, results soon surface. Team spirit rapidly becomes a resource to be drawn upon in times of slackness, confusion or stress by all team members, including the team leader, as I've found to my own surprise. A long time ago, as Scottish national coach, I took a very young volleyball team to the European Championships for the first time. One morning we arrived on time at the sportshall for a scheduled training session, only to find that the strong Israeli team were still on court. We waited a while but as they showed no sign of stopping, I caught the coach's eye and pointed to my wrist. The coach nodded but nothing happened. Gradually it became clear that, viewing us as complete outsiders (which we were), they weren't going to take any notice of us. I talked angrily to the coach but he moved away. The Israelis went on playing. I knew it was up to me to find a solution but I had no idea what to do. I felt embarrassed, furious and humiliated.

At that moment I noticed that my players had tired of waiting and were moving around lazily at the end of the hall, a volleyball at their feet. As I watched, their game became noisier and faster. They spread out and were soon passing the ball around the court itself. In no time, they were amongst the Israelis who angrily tried to push them away. When this failed the Israelis tried to take the ball but the Scots, relatively new to volleyball, proved to be masters of the ball at their feet. The Israelis gave up training and tried to tackle the Scots to gain possession. By this time the hall had become a football pitch, with the Scots shouting happily to each other. In five long minutes the Israelis failed to make any contact with the ball and eventually left the hall in relatively good humour. Our team had given a masterly display.

From this I learned that, even as coach, I did not always have to lead, did not always have to be right, did not always have to be in charge. Together we had created a strong team spirit and now I was fully entitled to draw on it too. That night our spirits were higher than at any point since our arrival and, in our first match, we did so well against the reigning champions that the Italian press were as interested in our post-match comments as they were in those of our opponents.

CHAPTER NINE

Children in Sport

Misia Gervis

As parents become more conscious of health-related fitness, there is more reason to get their children off the sofa and into the gym. This has resulted in a change in the image of sport and also in the expectations of parents. The question that needs to be addressed is how can we ensure that children experience a positive and pleasurable involvement in sport which will continue past their teens and into adult life?

The aims of this chapter are threefold. First, to explore sport from the child's perspective, to understand the potential sport has for the constructive development of young people, and to highlight the possible pitfalls that participation in sport can create. Second, to evaluate sport from the parental perspective. Why should parents encourage their children to be active in sport? What is the role of the coach in encouraging parents to be supportive? And third, we will be looking at the part a coach plays in the creation of a good atmosphere during training, and the relationship that the coach has with parents of young athletes. Clearly, the relationship between the young athlete, parents and coach is crucial. Consequently, we shall explore the integration of these roles.

Sport from the Child's Point of View

Ideally a child taking part in organized sport will be able to develop skills and abilities which will be of use in adult life. Such skills are often referred to as 'character builders' but the way in which they are acquired is now being questioned. It is no longer acceptable to expect children's sport to mirror in every detail adult sport. Children are qualitatively different from adults, and thus their expectations and needs from sport will differ considerably. Also all children should have the right to participate in sport at a level that is commensurate with their age and ability. This is the first crucial element that should be considered when viewing sport from the child's perspective.

The majority of sport that people are exposed to is through

the media, where the athletes are generally professionals, and consequently their behaviour will reflect this. Too often adults involved in children's sports, whether they be coaches, parents or officials, expect children's behaviour to mirror that of adult sport. Clearly this is inappropriate as it does not allow the children personal growth, but rather forces them to be adults too soon.

In professional sport there is the element of the entertainer – athletes have a job to do that often extends beyond the football pitch or track. It is all too easy for adults to expect children to behave in a similar way, but young athletes must be allowed to play as children for their pleasure, not for the entertainment of adults.

The majority of the young people who take part in sport will not become champions, even if their parents and coaches want this to happen. Most children have a wide variety of motives for taking part in sport, most of which are not related to winning but sheer enjoyment.

The way in which children feel about themselves is referred to as self-esteem. High self-esteem describes children who feel able to cope with the pressures around them. Low self-esteem is often associated with under-achievement and a poor self-image. This can develop if the coach is unaware that everyone in their training session needs to feel successful, and modifies sessions towards this end. Remember that children enjoy being able to master skills, and feel competent. They also enjoy doing new and exciting skills. Sport provides ample opportunity to do both.

Children also become involved in sport for social reasons. Their friends might invite them to a sports club, and they may enjoy participating in team games. Consequently sport provides the forum for the development of leadership skills and relationships, involving team mates and coaches.

All are valuable skills to learn as they are necessary for success in adult life. However, these qualities can only be nurtured within the right sporting context. It is therefore important that we understand how sport can be used constructively to aid children. Obviously the key person in ensuring that there is a positive, healthy atmosphere is the coach. The coach is often instrumental in determining continued participation by young athletes. Consequently, the coach needs to be aware of factors which can make physical activity enjoyable.

Helping Children Take Part

As we have already pointed out, children must be treated differently to adults. There are a number of ways in which coaches can make it easier for children to participate. For example, modification of rules and equipment might ensure that there is a greater playing time, and reduced frustration. For example, by lowering the height of a basketball hoop, small children will be more likely to score a basket, or by reducing the playing area in a game of football, children will not get so tired, and therefore will be able to concentrate more on their skills. In both these situations, they will gain more satisfaction. Most governing bodies of sport have now become alerted to this fact and are developing mini versions of their sport, which are well worth investigating.

Types of training and the length of a session can also be modified to children's needs. So, for example, with the very young, practice sessions need to be short but full of variety. As the children become older and more experienced, they can be longer and can focus on specific elements of performance. There are many simple practical things that coaches can do with a little creativity, which will increase the activity time for children. After all, children like to be active, and if they are not doing something, they can easily become bored and often drop out of sport altogether. By re-evaluating the sessions, coaches can develop very happy and skilled young athletes.

Children and Competition

There has been a lot of concern recently that there is too much emphasis on competition in children's sports to the detriment of the participants. Critics maintain that we should completely eliminate competitive sports because of the stress placed on participants. They would rather see co-operative sports where there are no winners or losers.

The underlying belief here is that competition leads to hostility and frustration, whereas co-operation encourages and develops trust and friendships. However, the situation is more complex than this and it is the way competition is used within the context of children's sport that is important.

In its simplest form competition merely provides us with a means of assessing and comparing our own abilities against others, something which occurs constantly in everyday life. However, the emphasis is on how we compete. The problems often emerge when there is an overwhelming emphasis on the

How can we ensure that children experience a positive and pleasurable partnership with sport which will continue past their teens and into adult life?

outcome or winning in sport. This is a limited view of competition which alienates many people. The real pleasure in competition is the striving for success.

Without wanting to win people would probably not participate in competition. Should we therefore embrace the ideal that winning is not the only thing, but that striving to win is very important? Another important factor is that the achievement of goals in training and practice are often more fulfilling than the competition itself. That is why you find young ice skaters on the ice at 5am, and runners putting in hundreds of miles in training.

Clearly, success must be forthcoming through these gruelling training times. But we must remember that success is not the same as winning. This is the message that must come across clearly from sports educators and parents. Evidently, this goes against what children experience about winning from watching television and often from ill-informed coaches and parents.

Another idea that needs to be rejected is the belief that you can only be a success at someone else's expense. The fact that that there are very few winners but an awful lot of losers, does not mean that most children cannot be successes. Being a success means achieving more than you did last time, or attaining personal goals rather than simply focusing on the outcome. In simple, practical terms this can mean swimming a lap one second faster than last month; sticking that vault in competition in the same way as in training; or making sure that you talk to your teammates on the pitch. If a young athlete has achieved a personal goal, then they will feel successful, which is the primary objective. A gold medal is not the one and only objective.

It is important that this distinction is recognized and fully appreciated by the adults who work with children in competitive sports. As we have already mentioned, children feel good about themselves when they have a positive self-image, and sport can provide this if the competitive element is handled well.

Let us now examine some of the potential problems associated with children, and how many of them can be minimized.

Competitive Stress

The following are the factors that make competition potentially stressful for young athletes.

Environment

These are factors that relate to the situation or environment of the competition, for example:

1.   The number of people watching the competition; large crowds are perceived as being more threatening than small crowds.
2.   Playing at home compared with playing away. This problem can be magnified if the competition is taking place in a foreign country.
3.   Playing in freezing cold conditions, or alternatively, playing in very hot weather.

These are all factors which might contribute to an athlete's fears and worries about the forthcoming competition.

People

These are factors that are related to the people who are involved with the athlete either before, during, or after the competition has taken place. Often the attitude of these people towards the athlete and the competition can have a big influence on stress. The people concerned are: the coach, teammates, friends, other competitors, and PARENTS. So, for example, a coach stressing the importance of victory at all costs might very well add to feelings of stress.

Athletes

These are the factors which relate to the athletes themselves. Such factors are internal and include the level of self-esteem, the level of importance they place on the competition, predisposition to anxiety (in level of trait anxiety), and their own expectations of success.

   All these different factors contribute to the perception of competitive stress, and can be summarized in the following way:

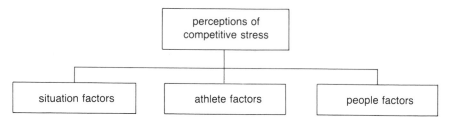

Fig 37   Factors contributing to perceptions of competitive stress.

It is clear that every athlete will view each and every competition differently. Consequently what is potentially stressful for one child will not be a problem for another. Nevertheless, there are similarities felt by all participants. The question is how can competitive stress be reduced?

One of the key factors in reducing stress is to shift the emphasis away from the outcome of the competition towards the performance. Children need constant recognition of their own abilities, and they should not be left to compare themselves to other athletes. By giving the athlete feedback about the positive element of their performance, and eliminating negative thoughts, the athlete will feel more confident.

Confident athletes feel in control of themselves, and therefore less stressed. Fear and self-doubt are often the fuels for competitive stress. Coaches can work on this approach to their sport in training and in competition. Another important factor that coaches can work on to reduce stress, involves ensuring that both they and their athletes have realistic expectations. If young athletes are not realistic about their own ability, it can lead to disappointment.

Children often get false ideas of their potential from adults. Sometimes the parents have inflated expectations, and sometimes the coaches. Either way it can be a potential source of stress for the child if they can't live up to these expectations.

And finally, the fun element must be constantly emphasized. Children must enjoy competing in sport to ensure their continued participation.

Exercise 26

Consider the following examples and try to predict how the parents' values might be reflected in the young athlete's attitude towards their sport:

1. Mr Jones is a badminton coach at the local sports centre. He coaches mainly recreational level badminton for people who want to stay healthy, but not really for high level competition. His daughter is involved in the volleyball team which trains at the same centre. She plays twice a week and also competes for the team:

ATTITUDES TOWARDS SPORT HELD BY PARENTS:

POSSIBLE EFFECTS OF PARENTAL VALUES ON THE YOUNG ATHLETE'S ATTITUDE AND PARTICIPATION IN SPORT:

2. Mr and Mrs Smith do not like sport, they never watch it on television considering it to be a waste of time. They are both overweight but do not appear to be overly concerned about this. They have a son who is a talented rugby player and who plays for the school team:

ATTITUDES TOWARDS SPORT HELD BY PARENTS:

POSSIBLE EFFECTS OF PARENTAL VALUES ON THE YOUNG ATHLETE'S ATTITUDE AND PARTICIPATION IN SPORT:

3. Mrs Black is a national ranked judge in gymnastics. She has been involved in the sport at the highest levels for many years. Most weekends are spent at competitions or at training sessions. She has a daughter who has grown up in the gym since she was a toddler. She has only known this way of life. She is now old enough at eight to begin competing:

ATTITUDES TOWARDS SPORT HELD BY PARENTS:

POSSIBLE EFFECTS OF PARENTAL VALUES ON THE YOUNG ATHLETE'S ATTITUDE AND PARTICIPATION IN SPORT:

4.   Mr White is a strong believer in children being able to stand up for themselves. He has a son who is considered to be a bit of a weakling, so he sends him to the local boxing club where he can be taught how to stand on his own two feet and not be afraid of anyone:

ATTITUDES TOWARDS SPORT HELD BY PARENTS:

POSSIBLE EFFECTS OF PARENTAL VALUES ON THE YOUNG ATHLETE'S ATTITUDE AND PARTICIPATION IN SPORT:

Parents

The values that children hold to be true about sport are first generated and reinforced by their parents. Parents will act as a powerful role model which will be reflected in the importance that is placed on the involvement in sport. This will obviously have an influence on how children perceive their own participation in sport.

Evidently in all the examples in **Exercise 26**, the parents hold certain values about sport which will be transmitted either directly or indirectly to their children. Along with these values they also have expectations as to what their child will be able to gain from their participation. Coaches also need to be aware of the motives of the parents and the children because it will have a direct effect on how that athlete will train.

In effect parents have reasons or motives for their children participating in sport. It is often these underlying motives which can be a potential source of conflict between parent and child if they are not fully considered or understood. If you as a coach are aware that a child is only attending your session to satisfy their parents' desires, you will not get the same input compared with children who are there to satisfy their own needs.

There are a wide range of participation mot   which are incentives to involvement in sport. These inclu   ch factors as: social, winning, fame, health, competing, money, medals/ trophies, gaining skills, and enjoyment.

Exercise 27

Try to analyse your own motives – or those of parents of children at your club – for involving a child in sport. Now, also consider the reasons why children might participate in sport. Compare the examples with your own or the parents' motives for involving young people in sport. Next, ask children why they feel that they want to be involved:

PARENTS' PARTICIPATION MOTIVES	CHILDREN'S PARTICIPATION MOTIVES

If you find that there is a mismatch between the adult's expectations and the child's, then it is worth reconsidering your own behaviour towards the child's involvement in sport. It is perhaps worthwhile at this point to remember that a child should not be playing to satisfy adult ambitions, but rather to fulfil their own. Furthermore, children are active in sport for their own pleasure and enjoyment, and this is what will fuel their interest in sport.

Understanding Motivation in Sport

To understand fully these motives which we have been discussing, we need to examine more closely the concept of motivation in relation to sport and how it affects young athletes' persistance. The following information links up closely with that covered in Chapter 2.

Essentially, there are two types of motivation which are derived from different sources. These are referred to as extrinsic and intrinsic motivation. Let us first examine extrinsic motivation. This refers to factors beyond the athlete which are influential in maintaining the athlete's interest in training and/or playing. Such factors can also be thought of as rewards.

Factors contributing to extrinsic motivation can be further distinguished as being either tangible or non-tangible. For example, a trophy given to the most improved player of the season is a tangible extrinsic reward. It immediately conveys a strong positive message to the receiver of the trophy that their efforts throughout the season have been noted and rewarded. When an athlete receives approval from a coach for a skill performed well this is a non-tangible extrinsic reward. Another type of this reward can be activity related. So, for example, the opportunity to have a fun activity after a hard session of drills might be given as a non-tangible extrinsic reward.

It is clear therefore that coaches and parents can sometimes be instrumental in giving children extrinsic rewards. For example, a parent expressing an interest in how a practice session went might well serve as a source of extrinsic motivation, and therefore help maintain the athletes interest in sport. However, there is often an over-emphasis on tangible rewards which can ultimately result in a child feeling over pressured to 'produce the goods'.

A classic example involves a parent offering a tangible reward for a certain performance. 'If you win your race today, I'll give you £10.' Although this is a reward, it is being offered in a very dangerous way and if the child fails to give the parent what they want, they have in effect failed twice, once in the competition and once in the eyes of the parents.

Exercise 28

Consider the types of rewards which you give to children involved in sport. Make a list and try to distinguish between different types. Do you tend to rely more on tangible or non-tangible rewards?

Coaches and parents who have a limited view of success, only being able to measure it in terms of tangible rewards, miss the point of sport. A remark I once heard by a father at a gymnastics competition, when his daughter had just won the bronze medal at her first British Championships, went as follows: 'Is that all you could manage?' This clearly demonstrates the damage that parents can cause if they only look at the extrinsic factors in sport.

Let us now turn our attention to intrinsic motivation. This refers to sources of motivation that stem from within the athlete. They include such factors as self-satisfaction, enjoyment, and feeling good about oneself. It is these rewards that really need to be emphasized because these are powerful in the long-term commitment to sport.

If young athletes are not intrinsically motivated, then they will not be fulfilled, and consequently will probably drop out. Research has indicated that one of the primary reasons children leave sport is because they are not enjoying themselves, and that they are not able to meet their need for self-fulfilment.

Athletes who only take part for the extrinsic rewards are never really satisfied, and will never fully enjoy themselves. One only has to think of the thousands of children who make sacrifices like getting up at 5am to take part in a swimming training session, or the young athletes who freely give up their weekends for practice time, to appreciate that they must be getting more out of it than the few tangible rewards that are on offer.

Parents and coaches therefore can help to foster intrinsic rewards and thus intrinsic motivation by placing greater emphasis on these aspects of sporting involvement.

For young athletes to have a positive experience of taking part in any sporting activity, they must be safe in the knowledge that they are actively supported by their parents. Even if parents do not share a love for that particular sport, it is very important that they find out enough about the sport to be actively interested. It can be very disheartening for a child to be involved in a sport knowing that the parents do not take it very seriously, and do not really support them.

Simple things such as turning up to watch the odd practice session, or watching competitions, give children a greater sense of security. This will be reflected in their attitude towards sport. Given that early participation in sport can lead to a life-style which is healthy and active, surely it is worthwhile to encourage children in their endeavours.

Another way in which parents can help to promote children's involvement is by understanding the rules. Here the coach can help perhaps by giving all parents a guide presentation to the sport. Encourage them to ask questions. If they are knowledgeable, they will probably be more supportive.

The Coach and the Parents

The third section of this chapter addresses the relationship between parents and coaches. This is often a source of conflict for those involved. Coaches tend to feel that the parents present a major problem, whereas parents sometimes feel that the coaches do not fully understand the needs of the children. However, the relationship between the coach and parents of young athletes is an important one if the child is to gain the most from sport. There still needs to be considerable respect from both parties, especially if the children are involved in competitive sport. There are several potential problems that can exist between parents and coaches which include:

1.   Parents becoming side-line coaches. This is where the parents are all too eager to offer their opinion about what a child is doing wrong. This will obviously undermine the work of the coach, and probably lead to hostility. This may spill over into the relationship the coach has with the athlete. Parents need to appreciate that the coach has the knowledge and expertise, and consequently they must trust the coach with their child.
2.   Coaches who exclude parents completely from the club. Coaches need to be aware that parents are their lifeline to their athletes. Without their commitment and co-operation, the children would not turn up at competitions or practice sessions. Therefore, coaches must ensure that they keep lines of communication open at all times between themselves and parents. If parents are given a considerable amount of information, then they will be more likely to co-operate. This can take the form of giving advance warning of practice sessions and competitions.

Coaches need to appreciate that parents have to juggle their own schedules around a child's. A daughter may be in the hockey team, the son learning music. Consequently if a coach suddenly announces two or three days beforehand that there is a team practice, they should not be surprised if there is a negative reaction from disgruntled parents who have already made other arrangements.

Parents also need to be able to feel that they can discuss their child's progress and development. The coach must be sensitive to these inquiries and make time available to deal with them in an appropriate manner. If coaches have the full support of the parents, it will make their job a lot easier.

This chapter has examined participation by children in sport from a number of different perspectives. Essentially there are three elements, the child, the coach and the parent. It is the coach who is the link. Consequently, the coach is very powerful in determining what kind of experience the child has. Involvement in sport should be one of the most positive aspects of a person's childhood, and this can be achieved if there is an awareness of the issues raised in this chapter. Ultimately, sport for children must give pleasure, not anxiety or stress. Through co-operation, communication and understanding, we should be able to produce confident, happy and skilful athletes.

CHAPTER TEN

Burnout

Dr Adrian Taylor

Acceptance that someone is burnt out is contrary to the popular macho expression 'when the going gets tough, the tough get going.' To admit to, or even contemplate, being under stress or burnt out may invite people to question our capabilities. How many of us would really not care about such a threat to our egos? This chapter is not about openly admitting our weaknesses to anyone. Instead it is written to give greater insight into how the demands of sport may influence both performance and relationships with others, and in the long term, dropout from participation or unfulfilled potential. It is written for all involved in sport at every level, including competitive and recreational, and the coaching, refereeing and administrative side.

For those sceptical about the existence of stress or burnout let me begin with two brief illustrative scenarios.

Scenario 1

Jane had been a successful swimmer throughout her adolescent years. She began to win local galas at the age of 10. Motivated by this early success and growing enthusiasm from her parents, coach and those around her, more and more of her time became devoted to swimming. Each competition was something to look forward to and then enjoy with frequent feelings of accomplishment. By the age of 13 Jane was as determined as ever.

Yet the long hours in the pool necessary to maintain her form at an increasingly competitive level were becoming tedious, particularly as school friends began to spend more time doing other things. School work also began to compete for her time but somehow she maintained the twice daily training routine amounting to over 20 hours a week in the pool. Her parents began to notice a change in the way Jane enjoyed success, particularly after achieving a regional gold medal for under sixteen year olds in the 50m breaststroke. It was as if she was becoming automated and just going through the motions with little pleasure or emotion.

In the following year instead of continuing to improve, a series of poor performances pointed to a problem. She trained harder than ever for her coach and to fulfil her goal, a medal at the Nationals, but she appeared to have lost something. Instead of enthusiastically supporting her teammates at the poolside she became withdrawn. Often tired, listless and finding concentration difficult, her schoolwork also began to suffer. Just before the National Championships a visit to Jane's doctor, following a few weeks of sore throats and colds, produced a diagnosis of glandular fever.

After a six-week period away from exercise Jane realized that her love for swimming had gone. She associated the swimming pool with hard training and an impersonal place with little time to enjoy the company of others. Although she kept in contact with some people at the club and had fully recovered from her illness, two years later Jane had not been near a pool.

Scenario 2

Geoff had worked as a teacher at a large school for 15 years. Shortly after arriving at the school his natural interest in football had been strongly encouraged. He had accumulated responsibilities to the point where every moment of his day was spoken for: lunch was eaten while his school football team changed for practice or while supervising children in the playground. After school he was usually to be seen coaching or refereeing one of the school football teams.

Following an injury Geoff had taken on the role as assistant coach, and was now coach with the local semi-professional team. They trained three evenings a week and played each Saturday for 10 months of the year, often having to travel three hours for away games. On Sundays there was a regional schoolboys team to coach, a responsibility which also added to the long list of committee meetings that Geoff had to attend. During school holidays Geoff was central to the organization of local football camps for 12–16 year olds. It would be fair to say that life revolved around football.

For the past few years those around Geoff had been noticing a change in the formerly relaxed, confident and warm character. Geoff was not aware of anything. As a perfectionist he had always expected the most from those he coached and his enthusiasm usually resulted in just that. Five years earlier some changes had taken place at work which left Geoff with the feeling that his efforts were not appreciated. With less enthusiasm for

Athletes may experience psychological burnout when under intense pressure for some time.

the school teams Geoff took less interest in the children and became more detached. A coach previously full of praise and encouragement slowly became cynical and negative towards his players. He expressed more criticism and noticed fewer positive events. An autocratic coaching style spread to the men's senior team and in turn Geoff gained less respect and poor results. Increasingly he became irritable and in moments of high tension confronted referees, opposition, spectators and even his own players.

In his earlier years as a coach Geoff had attended coaching clinics and keenly read about all aspects of the game. Now he appeared unreceptive to new ideas and had gained little from the past five years. Instead, he appeared to have gone through the same year five times, repeating errors as a coach and failing to avoid unnecessary conflict with others.

These examples are not uncommon in sporting circles. They appear to be very different and yet in many ways there is overlap in the way sport engulfed two very dedicated people. It is quite common for people suffering from burnout to be unaware that they have changed in any way and this adds to the difficulty of doing anything about it.

Let us next look at the signs and symptoms of burnout in more detail, and later focus on the causes and consequences. Finally, we shall turn to some suggestions for controlling the development of burnout and rekindling enthusiasm.

What is this State Called Burnout?

Research has predominantly focused on occupations which involve work with other people, such as teaching, nursing, social work, policing, etc. In this sense burnout may best be labelled psychological burnout whereby an individual becomes emotionally exhausted from constant giving or caring for others. Burnout can also affect coaches, physical education teachers, referees, physiotherapists and others who are intensely committed to their role, as either professionals or amateurs. Athletes too may experience psychological burnout when under intense pressure for some time. High attrition rates among junior athletes with considerable potential, and a growing shortage of referees in fast moving team games, have suggested that sport also involves physical burnout.

Burnout has been described as a progressive loss of idealism, energy and purpose. The loss of physical and emotional energy may also be accompanied by negative attitudes, and the belief that less is being accomplished. In later stages of burnout there is commonly a decline in interest to the point where complete withdrawal or dropout takes place. Not everyone leaves sport due to burnout of course. People often move on to other sports and activities because they believe the personal rewards may be greater. Such changes should be viewed as development not burnout. However, when athletes like Jane become repelled by an activity which once provided a deep source of personal satisfaction, this is serious.

Two elements of burnout have been identified. First is psychological burnout.

Psychological Burnout

The questions in **Exercise 29** may give further insight into the nature of this kind of burnout. In the past six months how often have you experienced the feelings described in each statement. Substitute your sporting role (eg., player, coach, referee, etc.) in the spaces provided. Complete **Exercise 29**.

Exercise 29

VERY OFTEN	OFTEN	SOMETIMES	RARELY	NEVER
4	3	2	1	0

MENTAL EXHAUSTION (ME)

1. I feel less inclined to plan and think about what I am doing than when I began as a . . . .   _____

2. I am so emotionally tired after a competition that I cannot recall much about it.   _____

3. I feel mentally tired before beginning a training session.   _____

4. I find small problems more frustrating than they used to be.   _____

ME SCORE   _____

DEPERSONALISATION (DE)

1. I find myself treating others rather impersonally and feel less sensitive and more hardened towards others.   _____

2. When things go wrong I am less tolerant as a . . . . and tend to blame others more than I used to.   _____

3. I feel that I am often blamed for the errors or failure of others, as a . . . .   _____

4. As a . . . . I am not concerned about the personal achievements of others as much as I used to be.   _____

DE SCORE   _____

PERSONAL ACCOMPLISHMENT (PA)

1. As a . . . . I don't feel that I am accomplishing as much as I used to.   _____

2. When I began as a . . . . I felt that I could make more impact than I feel I do now.   _____

3. I don't feel that I need to achieve as much now as when I began as a . . . .   _____

4. As a . . . . I don't seem to hold the same respect among those around me that I have always held.   _____

PA SCORE   _____

TOTAL BURNOUT SCORE   _____

A total burnout score of less than 20 suggests that you have lost little personal satisfaction from your involvement, you are full of energy and enthusiasm for your sport, and maintain excellent relations with others. Total scores of between 20–35 may indicate that you are in the early or middle stages of burnout. A total burnout score of over 35 indicates that you may seriously need to consider your involvement in sport, and how to return to a position which once demanded less and/or provided more perceived rewards.

Now go back and examine which aspects of burnout appear to be most developed. A score of 10 or more for any one of the three burnout components (ME, DE, PA) requires attention.

A high ME score suggests that you may be out of control. Instead of carefully setting goals or plans you are so emotionally tired that things just happen in an automated way. It is difficult to learn from experience in this state since you may miss much of what actually goes on, or you only focus on specific aspects of problems: you cannot see the forest for the trees. Overtraining is a good example in which, as you earlier saw with Jane, it may be hard to see how taking a break could help. People in this category often have difficulty in saying 'No', and may feel inadequate if they are seen to be slowing down. Mental exhaustion may also affect the way we interact.

A high DE score suggests that you have changed in the way you get on with others. The development of negative attitudes and cynicism is a common subconscious way of detaching oneself from relationships. While some people may become withdrawn and often silent in social situations, others may become easily irritated and angry. In sports roles such as coaching, which require a keen interest and understanding of each athlete, the effects of developing feelings of DE can be particularly inhibiting, as we saw with Geoff. Autocratic coaching styles often develop which involve poor personal relations and limited trust between coach and athlete. Mental energy is usually necessary to develop and maintain positive relations with others. It is therefore common for feelings of depersonalization to coincide with mental tiredness or exhaustion.

A high PA score suggests that although you may still be putting as much into your sporting activity, the personal rewards do not seem as high as they once did. Are you over involved, as Geoff appeared to be earlier? Again this may result from a difficulty in saying 'No'. Another example involves a severe shortage of referees or officials. Those involved tend to do more and more, often resulting in a decreased feeling of personal accomplishment. Despite continued success we may also increasingly attribute

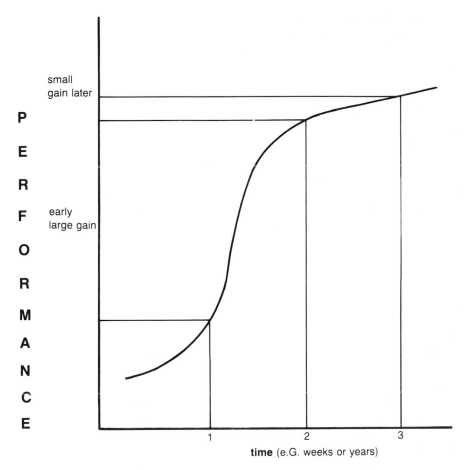

Fig 38 Law of diminishing returns.

our accomplishments to luck, others on our team, or poor performances by opponents. It is of course quite natural to achieve relatively less as we become more proficient at something. **Figure 38** demonstrates the Law of Diminishing Returns in which our improvements in some sporting skills, such as shooting in basketball or canoeing down a river, are quite noticeable in the early stages of learning but then diminish as we reach a higher level of performance. With reference to our earlier example, Jane had to come to terms with putting more than ever into sport as she improved but felt the rewards were diminishing.

Unless an athlete can overcome the frustration from this apparent lack of progress, feelings of reduced personal accomplishment may result. Setting clear goals to prepare ourselves for realistic achievement is one way to overcome this frustration.

Obviously there will be differences between the way each

person feels about what they are doing. What is important is the way in which your feelings have changed, and many of the statements reflect this. If you were to complete the survey again in a few years time, feelings about your involvement may have stayed the same or changed. Awareness of change in a negative direction, as we shall discuss later, is an excellent starting point in combating the development and symptoms of burnout.

There are many other psychological symptoms which may also be present, but are not exactly part of burnout. For example, athletes may experience a lack of motivation, depression, increased anxiety, irritability and loss of concentration. Because burnout develops from prolonged periods of stress, these and other symptoms which are often associated with stress, may become evident.

Physical Burnout

Undoubtedly, physical and psychological burnout are related but as yet it is unclear how. Physical exhaustion may clearly influence the way in which we feel about ourselves and others. Our emotional state also has a considerable effect on how we physically feel.

Burnout also involves a physical component. Chronic fatigue syndrome has received increasing research attention following a variety of recent 'breakdowns' among top-level athletes. Sebastian Coe's disappointing exit from international competition at the 1990 Commonwealth Games and Steve Ovett's withdrawal from the 1984 Olympics in Los Angeles provide well-known examples. Despite careful monitoring of training progress, athletes have experienced viral infections associated with inhibition of the immune system and a greater susceptibility to illness. Physical burnout cannot simply be explained in terms of a plateau, as in the case of staleness, but rather a distinct lengthy decline in performance below anticipated levels based on previous training and attainment.

In this chapter the focus will largely be on psychological burnout because any reasonable account of the chronic fatigue syndrome must consider biochemical and hormonal changes which are beyond the scope of this book. However, the statements below may help to identify some of the characteristics of physical burnout.

Complete **Exercise 30** to gain your score for physical burnout.

Exercise 30

VERY OFTEN	OFTEN	SOMETIMES	RARELY	NEVER
4	3	2	1	0

PHYSICAL BURNOUT (PB)
(for active participants)

1. I feel more fatigued before training sessions than I used to do. _____
2. I feel physically exhausted after competitions. _____
3. On many days I feel heavy and tired. _____
4. I feel lethargic, weak and lack energy before competitions. _____
5. When I really push myself in competition I don't seem to have the extra gear I used to have. _____

PB SCORE _____

A PB score of 13 or more may indicate that you have been involved at a very intense level for too long. There is a difference between physical burnout and short-term fatigue, although the symptoms may appear the same. Short-term fatigue is particularly common when athletes return from injury or an unplanned lay-off, and rapidly increase (by more than say 15 per cent per week) their volume and/or intensity of physical exercise (ie, workload). Recovery may be fairly straightforward with an easier period of exercise over the following weeks.

Individual athletes such as runners, swimmers and cyclists can easily monitor their volume and intensity of exercise, but it is less easy for team athletes when the demands vary considerably from game to game. At the end of a hard season, the term flame-out has been used to describe the fatigue from which the body may also recover fairly rapidly with a break or reduction in exercise. On the other hand, physical burnout may reflect more permanent changes due to perhaps years of often unbroken periods of intense exertion. How long is the 'off-season' in your sport? It appears that some sports have extended their season to the point where it is almost possible to compete over the entire year. Has the length of season changed in your sport, and do you feel this has had any effect on you/the participants?

Physical burnout can be avoided by incorporating the following points into careful planning.

1.   The gradual build-up of involvement is vital, but how often do we ignore this simple rule? Players (and indeed active officials for team sports) often begin brief but intense pre-season training having done little for weeks. 'Off-seasons' should not involve total rest, but rather a less intense recovery period.
2.   Over-training and fatigue during the season can be avoided by mixing intense with lighter training sessions. This applies to all who train seriously, whether weightlifters, cyclists or rugby players. Note that some people find it difficult to train less intensely for certain sessions, which merely emphasizes the need for setting and abiding with training plans.
3.   Repeated or continuous physical over-loading of an athlete may, in the long term, result in burnout. It is therefore important to monitor progress carefully over time, be wary of early warning signs of fatigue, and cut back if necessary.

How Does Burnout Develop and Are You Susceptible?

Take any group of people and observe the physical and psychological differences between them. Our swimmer, Jane, eventually appeared to burn out from over-training while others no doubt continued to find the resources to meet the demanding training routine. Geoff, the coach, expended an enormous amount of emotional energy, over the years, on his students and players, before eventually over-loading himself with occupational and recreational demands. There are limits to everyone's physical and psychological resources (also called adaptation energy) which are important to recognize. The point at which someone reaches burnout will depend on the individual's energy reserves as can be seen in **Figure 39**.

Person A and B both experience a stressor of equal importance. The initial reaction is one of alarm or perhaps shock, and energy levels fall as both organize themselves to react to the stressor successfully. The stressor then acts as a challenge to engage a higher level of physical and psychological resources. After some period of resistance (weeks or years) energy levels are finally depleted and exhaustion, followed by burnout, develops. However, person A appears to have less adaptation energy for the continuing demands of the activity, and reaches burnout earlier than person B.

Those who are unable to recognize these limits, or who are unable to decline an offer to take on more, are perhaps most susceptible to burnout. Therefore burnout may develop from

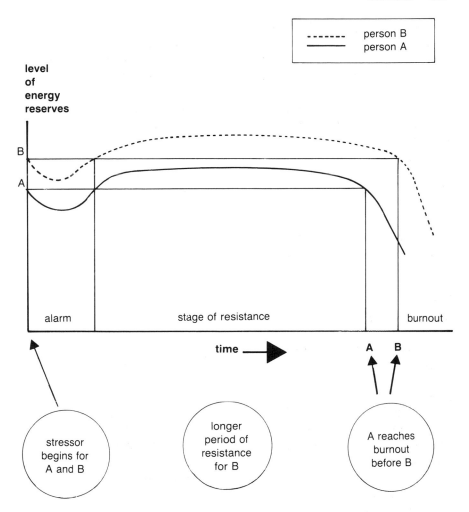

Fig 39   Adaptation energy, stress and burnout.

overloading our lives with physical and mental demands. In a society which places a strong emphasis on the work ethos, there is a popular belief in some sports that if a lot is good, then more will be better. Top level swimmers have at least doubled their training distance over the past 15 years and such demands are filtering down to young children. Long hours are also expected of young gymnasts. Among mature athletes, those involved in multi-event sports such as triathlons, decathlons and pentathlons may spend more time in training than any other group. The ability to limit involvement may be a vital characteristic to avoid burnout.

While decisions about involvement in sport would appear to rest on the individual, life may not always be so simple. There are external demands or pressures placed upon us that make such decisions very difficult, and almost beyond our control.

Since an athlete may play with various teams each week and come into contact with several coaches, each with their own interests at stake, it may be hard for a teenager to restrict time spent playing and practising. Intensive participation may also continue year-round where an athlete is involved in more than one activity. Few mature top-level athletes are able to maintain back-to-back seasons; it is more common for children to attempt to fulfil the demands of several sports in a single year.

Coaches should of course be very wary of their athletes' capabilities both in the short and long term. For example, a recent report recognized that some gifted teenage soccer players were playing over 150 matches a year. They appeared to be able to cope with the physical and psychological demands of school teams, local league teams and various representative teams up to national schoolboy level. However, the effects of such an intensive schedule over several years more often than not leads to symptoms of burnout. How often has the England soccer team played with a lack of inspiration and flair in past years?

I know of at least one professional soccer manager who carefully limits the number of games his son plays, but there are also many who play say five games a week for much of the year. The advent of summer leagues has added to the demands. Physical burnout may therefore result from physical stress, or in other words, an imbalance between a person's capabilities and the demands placed upon that person.

There is obviously a moral need for someone to take overall responsibility for susceptible young athletes and this occurs in some sports but not in others.

Does it occur in your sport?
If not can you think of a scheme to monitor total involvement,
other than parental guidance?

There is another type of person who may be more susceptible to psychological burnout. An extrinsically motivated individual, predominantly concerned with external rewards from participation (eg, trophies) may eventually devalue such honours. It is therefore important to gain satisfaction from simply participating (ie, intrinsic motivation). Switching the emphasis from extrinsic to intrinsic motives among children is a critical function of the coach if burnout is to be avoided in young athletes.

Perfectionists may also be susceptible to burnout. Do you have difficulty in delegating responsibilities to others when you feel that the only way something will be done properly is to do it yourself? Perfectionists often overload themselves with minor tasks, which may contribute to burnout.

In summary, the person most susceptible to burnout may be someone who:

1.   Is energetic with a strong need to be involved, and achievement oriented.
2.   May lack assertiveness in psychologically demanding situations and has difficulty in delegating or saying 'No'.
3.   Is involved largely for extrinsic type rewards, rather than for the intrinsic pleasure of participation.
4.   Likes to see things done to perfection.

Consequences of Burnout

Two highly likely scenarios follow the development of burnout:

1.   The person remains in that sport but continues to function at a level well below full mental and perhaps physical potential. Such people are not doing justice to themselves (as individuals or in fulfilling the demands of their sport), or to those around them if the success and enjoyment of others is in any way dependent on them (e.g. teammates, athletes being coached, etc).
2.   The person leaves the sport. If the departure is permanent then sport may lose a valuable competitor with a wealth of experience or unfulfilled potential. A more satisfactory outcome may evolve from a temporary break and return to normal functioning. Suggestions for recovering from burnout will be made later.

Neither of these outcomes is at all desirable, so it is important to prevent or avoid burnout from developing in the first place. The first step is through an understanding of how burnout may develop and this is where we turn next.

Stress and Burnout

Psychological stress occurs when perceived demands, threats or fears outweigh the perceived capabilities or benefits. Competitive sport involves a continuous series of battles against opponents and yourself. If we begin to see each battle as a threat rather than a challenge then competition becomes stressful. There is evidence that psychological burnout develops from prolonged periods of psychological stress, just as intense physical stress over several years may lead to physical burnout. As we noted above, physical and psychological fatigue and staleness from relatively short periods of stress are not likely to last as long as burnout symptoms.

Of course some stress is essential to motivate us to optimal performance (as discussed in Chapter 3) and an ideal state of well-being as shown in **Figure 40**. For many there would be no pleasure from sport without competition and challenge. We may initially become involved in an activity largely because of our perception of the degree of challenge involved (ie, the balance between demands and capabilities). For example, a rock climber or skier selects the degree of difficulty to gain what has been called eustress (positive stress) and avoid distress (negative stress).

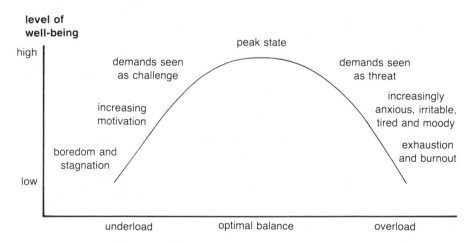

Fig 40   Stress and well-being.

Perhaps you can think of some words which may describe how you feel when in a peak well-being. Clearly, the greater the imbalance between perceived demands and perceived capabilities, the less positive we may feel. In extreme situations where the imbalance may be prolonged then continued involvement in that sport will be unlikely. But it is important to note that not everyone drops out of an activity because of burnout. In fact, boredom with one activity and interest in another is perhaps a more common reason why people change roles.

Sources of Psychological Stress

I'm sure that most of us could list various demands placed upon us at work or in school that may cause us some stress. These sources of stress are known as stressors and may also be found in sport. **Figure 41** shows some typical stressors for various roles in sport.

The list includes four stressors which are fairly common in sport, irrespective of the role we play.

The élite amateur athlete like Jane, the dedicated coach like Geoff, and many others, at all levels, wish to spend as much time as possible involved in their sport while working and maintaining other interests in life. Time pressures undoubtedly create frustration and social/family relations often suffer. And yet research suggests that it is the support from others that is often crucial in coping with stress and avoiding burnout. Researchers have labelled people with hurry sickness, who continually live under time pressure as they attempt to achieve more than seems possible, as Type 'A' personalities. Geoff may have been such a character. Perhaps you know someone who fits the description? Time pressures from attempting too much may undoubtedly contribute to burnout. It is important to note that amateur involvement in sport can be equally if not more demanding than for a professional.

Do you ever find yourself taking your frustrations out on others on the field? The battles mentioned earlier may become interpersonal conflicts which just add to the demands of sport. As burnout advances, such conflicts become more common, which in turn requires more adaptation energy or coping resources, bringing the stage of psychological exhaustion that bit closer.

Competition in sport is not always limited to the formal setting. Athletes compete for places on teams, administrators and coaches may jostle for better positions, and referees/officials may compete for more prestigious appointments or more senior certification. Some people are particularly adept at winning friends and influencing people, otherwise known as politics, while many find this aspect of sport a major turn-off.

STRESSOR	EXAMPLES
Sport in general:	
1. Time pressures	Work and social/family life do not leave enough time for your sport.
2. Interpersonal conflicts	Sport involves competition, but some just take it too far.
3. Politics	It is often not how good you are but who you know.
4. Fear of failure	A lot depends on how important doing well or winning is to you.
For the athlete:	
1. Lack of control/autonomy	Authoritarian coaches rarely consult athletes about things such as training plans.
2. Pressure from those around	The media and/or supporters seem to expect consistent brilliance. It may not be easy to train and compete when *you* want to.
3. Injury	All that training could be wasted in a split second.
For the coach:	
1. Role conflict	One minute you are everyone's listening ear, then you have to discipline your athletes: team selection is never easy when it is subjective.
2. Role ambiguity	Everyone expects you to develop winners but at what cost? Should you encourage gamesmanship?
3. Lack of support/respect	Sometimes nothing you do is appreciated, and there are many others who could do better.
4. Lack of autonomy	You would like to just get on with the job but there are always others who want to interfere.
5. Fear of dismissal	In some sports at certain levels 'winning isn't everything, it's the only thing'.
For the referee/umpire/official:	
1. Fitness concerns (for team sports)	It is getting harder each year to stay up with play.
2. Interpersonal conflicts	Some players, coaches and spectators seem intent on antagonizing the official.

3.	Lack of support/respect/recognition	Sometimes nothing you do is appreciated, and there always seem to be many others who could do better: the highest acclaim is often silence at the end of a game.
4.	Peer conflicts/politics	Even fellow officials can be quick to point out poor calls. Is promotion and match selection always conducted without bias?
5.	Fear of harm	There are a growing number of verbal and physical assaults.
6.	Fear of failure	Do you feel that one bad call can ruin a game or affect the outcome?

Fig 41   Typical sources of stress in sport.

Fear of failure has been identified as a leading source of stress among many involved in sport, particularly among the younger age groups and those at élite levels. Like the other stressors, a situation requires some interpretation before it becomes a source of stress. In this case, those who tend to place winning very highly, or who have committed most to succeeding and are also less confident in their own ability, are likely to be the ones who fear failure the most.

Other common sources of stress for athletes, coaches and officials are also shown in **Figure 41**. You may agree with some, or notice that the stressors that you find important are not listed.

Now it's your turn!
List five sources of stress which you find particularly important in the role you play in sport.

Of course most of us will learn to deal with stressors, or they may not be particularly enduring. As we saw earlier, they may even become a source of motivation. Burnout only develops from chronic stress in which an accumulation of stressors deplete our resources over a period of time. There are many ways in which we adapt to stress with differing success. In the following section some suggestions will be made for avoiding burnout through stress management and other techniques, but first why not briefly note one way in which you deal with each of the five stressors you listed above.

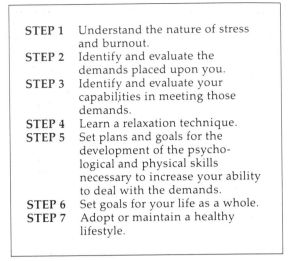

STEP 1	Understand the nature of stress and burnout.
STEP 2	Identify and evaluate the demands placed upon you.
STEP 3	Identify and evaluate your capabilities in meeting those demands.
STEP 4	Learn a relaxation technique.
STEP 5	Set plans and goals for the development of the psychological and physical skills necessary to increase your ability to deal with the demands.
STEP 6	Set goals for your life as a whole.
STEP 7	Adopt or maintain a healthy lifestyle.

Fig 42   Seven steps to avoid burnout.

Avoiding or Recovering from Burnout

There are various steps which may prevent the development or reverse the symptoms of burnout. These are listed in **Figure 42**.

Step 1: In reading this chapter you have already initiated Step 1. By understanding something about stress and burnout you are in a better position to take action, whether it is to control your own life or to help others.

Steps 2 and 3: Your sport may involve many demands, both physical and psychological. To avoid a build-up of continuous stress which may result in burnout it is important for you to identify those demands and recognize your own capabilities. Situations themselves are not psychological stressors; how we perceive them and cope with them is more important. Earlier, you may have listed the same psychological stressors as someone else, but for different reasons.

Using the same five stressors as before,
write down why they are stressful for you
in terms of demands and your capabilities.

It is important to assess your degree and type of involvement in the sporting role you play. Over-involvement may create the need to reduce the hours spent training or coaching. There may also be a need to examine the way you interact with others. As described in Chapter 7, coaches, for example, adopt a variety of leadership styles from the autocratic (ie, dominating) to total consideration. Research has linked the latter style, involving great concern for the feelings and well-being of others, with higher levels of burnout. If you predominantly adopt this style as a coach it may be advisable to become less approachable, thereby 'giving' less emotionally, to avoid burnout. Employing the support of others, such as parents, may also aid a move in this direction.

Step 4: There are many relaxation techniques used by athletes at all levels. While some sports, such as soccer, have been slow to recognize the need for stress control, nearly all present-day Olympians use some form of mental training for competition.

Relaxation training may involve the following: mental strategies, such as visualization of peaceful situations; physical strategies, such as progressive muscle relaxation or deep breathing; or a combination of the two, such as autogenic training. The latter involves the use of mental suggestion to influence physiological functioning. Other mental strategies include a reassessment of one's perceptions of stressors, and training in self-confidence and self-assertiveness. Each individual may find certain techniques to be more beneficial than others. It is therefore recommended that the reader gains further information about several, and then practises one technique regularly for optimum effect.

Step 5: Goal setting is an important strategy used to develop abilities and skills in an efficient and effective way. Having recognized the actual and perceived demands of an activity (both physical and psychological), short and long-term goals can be set for the development of the skills necessary to overcome those demands. For example, if an athlete is finding that the pressure to win before competition is draining or causing insomnia, then certain relaxation skills may be worth developing. Like physical skills, development takes place most effectively by setting dates when specific measurable targets will be attained. A coach should be able to help each athlete develop individual goals. In sport, the goals of a coach and athlete are sometimes incompatible which leads to disharmony. For example, if the motives for a player's involvement in sport are of a social nature and the coach is more achievement oriented then this can be considered in future planning. Open dialogue between coach and athlete is essential and can be a key factor in minimizing conflict and frustration, and in turn burnout.

Goal setting also involves the careful planning of weekly, seasonal and annual training/competition cycles. Such plans are essential to avoid over-training and burnout by providing clear, intensive, recovery periods.

Setting goals and taking an interest in your role in sport can help to maintain motivation, as explained in Chapter 2. A recommendation for avoiding burnout may therefore involve remaining actively involved in personal development, irrespective of the role you play. In addition to the rapidly growing number of books on all aspects of sport, there are regular practical and academic courses of varying length for all levels of participant. Are you up-to-date with physical and mental training techniques, dietary requirements, and injury prevention and treatment methods for your sport?

Step 6: Have you ever stopped to think about what you enjoy most about life? Do you live for your sport? If you have a family, how much time do you spend with them? Have you ever been frustrated by the lack of time to fulfil the demands of your occupation, family or social relations, and sporting interests? Burnout in sport cannot be entirely attributed to physical and psychological stress within sport. A broader perspective is important because our physical and psychological state is often transferred from one sphere to another. Remember, Jane was facing the extra pressures of exams when she left swimming, and Geoff changed following his lack of appreciation as a teacher.

Even with the best intentions, the plans you set out in Step 5 may come unstuck due to conflicting demands from work or family. Setting goals for your life will help avoid time pressure which contributes to burnout. Coaches of young athletes must be particularly concerned about this, as I discussed earlier. Extended involvement in sport without the full support of family members may also be a recipe for eventual burnout from sport or marital problems. Goal setting for life is therefore recommended, with priorities set to expend energy on a weekly, monthly and annual basis.

Step 7: There is little doubt that our overall well-being influences the way we react to the physical and psychological pressures of life, both in sport and elsewhere. A recent study led to questions being asked about the health of several top Rugby League referees. Their response to physical and psychological stressors suggested that they were in danger of coronary arrest while officiating, and were subsequently not used for professional matches. Obviously burnout is not life threatening, but maintenance of a healthy lifestyle can help to cope with the pressures of sport. Such healthy habits include adequate sleep, a balanced diet, regular aerobic-type exercise (even for coaches and administrators), not smoking, and limited caffeine and alcohol intake.

Now, while still thinking about the seven steps, write down five ways in which you can minimise the effects of stress either for yourself or one of your athletes, and thereby reduce the likelihood of physical or psychological burnout. Think of a new suggestion. Were any of the ways specifically related to dealing with the stressors you listed earlier?

Summary

The purpose of this chapter was to increase awareness of how sport may influence the way we feel about ourselves and others, particularly when faced with demands which may exceed our resources. You have been given the opportunity to analyse what factors contribute to stress in your sport. Stress and burnout can be controlled and seven steps were suggested. Although the excitement is what attracts many people to sport, it is hoped that the exercises presented here will enable you to gain more insight into the physical and psychological aspects of sport which may contribute to burnout.

CHAPTER ELEVEN

The Role of the Sport Psychologist

Dr Stephen J. Bull

In the Olympic games of 1976, for the first time a psychologist was assigned to the American team. It was not until 1984, however, that systematic services in sport psychology were provided to the American Winter and Summer Olympic teams. In recent years, however, the demand for sport psychology consultation from individual athletes and teams has increased enormously. In preparation for the 1988 Winter and Summer Olympics no less than 25 different sports in the American squad used a sport psychologist as part of their preparation programme. In Britain now there are at least 30 sport psychologists working in various sports including hockey, netball, rugby, croquet, cricket, gymnastics and tennis.

The popular image of a sport psychologist is of someone who essentially attempts to heighten athlete aggression and competitiveness prior to a big game. The psychologist is seen as teaching athletes how to develop that winning psychological edge, and how to use the killer instinct to its best advantage. Traditionally, the sport psychologist has been viewed as being the last resort to whom coach and athlete turn when performance has slumped, a problem-solver who is only brought in when things are going seriously wrong. These assumptions, however, have been misguided. Today the actual role of the sport psychologist is becoming known and appreciated. The purpose of this chapter is to describe the different functions and roles which sport psychologists can play in order that their contribution is more fully understood.

The Sport Psychologist

Most sport psychologists received their training in university departments of sports science, physical education, or psychology. They usually obtain a first degree in either a sport-related subject or psychology, and then study sport psychology at the masters and/or doctoral degree level.

It is initially important to explain that there are essentially two different roles for a sport psychologist to play – a practical consultancy and a scientific research role. Many individuals assume both roles at different times, although some remain strictly involved in only one capacity.

Practical Consultancy

In this context the main aim of a sport psychologist is to assist athletes in the development of psychological skills which facilitate both performance enhancement as well as enjoyment and satisfaction. The skills outlined in Chapter 6 typify the work carried out by practical sport psychologists. They teach athletes techniques for coping with stress and anxiety, strategies for improving concentration, methods of maintaining motivation and ways of enhancing self-confidence. In an athlete's overall programme of training and preparation, the mental side complements the technical, tactical and physical components which are usually handled by the coach and trainer. In this way the sport psychologist can become a valuable member of the coaching team, not replacing any other member of the coaching staff, but providing an additional element which can often allow the other three components to be expressed successfully.

Many, although not all, sport psychologists are lecturers at universities, polytechnics and colleges. They teach undergraduate and graduate students in physical education and sports science. They are usually experienced athletes themselves and have sometimes coached their chosen sport(s).

Before reading on, pause for a moment and complete **Exercise 31**.

Exercise 31

Consider the role a practical sport psychologist might play in your sport. What are the mental skills most appropriate to your sport and how could a sport psychologist become part of your 'coaching team'?

Some sport psychologists have training and qualifications in clinical psychology and are hence licensed/chartered clinical psychologists. Individuals with this background and expertise sometimes have an important role to play as practical sport psychologists since they are well placed to help athletes deal with emotional and personality problems which may arise. Clinical problems which arise in the sporting environment include alcohol and drug abuse, relationship difficulties (between coach and athlete, parents and athlete, or spouse and athlete, etc), eating disorders, and severe depression. These are problems for which most sport psychologists are not trained, and the skills and expertise of a clinically trained individual are therefore needed.

Before reading on, pause for a moment and complete **Exercise 32**.

Exercise 32

Consider the role a sport psychologist with clinical training might play in your sport. Can you think of any individuals in your experience who may have benefited from the skills offered by this type of professional?

The role of a sport psychologist with clinical training is less prominent and such skills are less frequently employed in most sporting contexts. The majority of athletes from all sports can benefit from education in the application of mental skills training, but the number who require clinical help is much less. Nevertheless, access to a clinically trained sport psychologist is a valuable asset to a coaching network because the individual can be used if and when needed.

Scientific Research

Although much less visible, the role of a research sport psychologist is a very important one. The credibility of the practical sport psychologist depends on the scientific body of knowledge accumulated by researchers. Research sport psychologists are interested in investigating the factors which influence behaviour and performance in sport. In other words, they undertake research experiments in the psychology of sport and physical activity itself. These experiments are sometimes carried out in a laboratory, sometimes in a gymnasium, and sometimes at sporting venues when competition is actually occurring. The research sport psychologist makes use of a range of different methods and equipment, including laboratory apparatus (such as reaction timers and heart-rate monitors), as well as observation techniques for monitoring behaviour patterns (for instance

It is the responsibility of the sport psychologist to become involved in the athlete's training and competition rather than always operating from an office.

how often an aggressive act is committed during a particular period of play).

One of the most common forms of investigation is through the use of questionnaires. A number of different questionnaires are regularly used in sport psychology research, and one of the most popular ones was discussed in Chapter 3. The Sport Competition Anxiety Test (SCAT) was developed by Rainer Martens in 1977. It measures competitive trait anxiety, and there is a children's as well as adult version. Martens and his colleagues also developed another very popular questionnaire in 1982. The Competitive State Anxiety Inventory-2 (CSAI-2) measures state anxiety in sport, and it assesses three different dimensions – worry, physiological arousal, and self-confidence.

The Test of Attentional and Interpersonal Style (TAIS) was developed in 1976 by Robert Nideffer. It measures a person's attention characteristics and skills in different types of concentration. The Causal Dimension Scale (CDS) assesses athletes' perceived causes for results, and relates closely to the material covered in Chapter 5. The questionnaire was developed by Dan Russell in 1982 and is used by researchers investigating attribution theory.

The Psychological Skills Inventory for Sports (PSIS) is a wide ranging questionnaire which measures a number of different factors. It was developed by Michael Mahoney and his colleagues in 1987 and assesses the skills of anxiety management, concentration, self-confidence, motivation, mental preparation and team emphasis. A similar test developed by two British sport psychologists, Dave Nelson and Lew Hardy, in 1989 is the Sport-related Psychological Skills Questionnaire (SPSQ). This measures skills in imagery, mental preparation, self-confidence, anxiety management, concentration, relaxation and motivation.

The Group Environment Questionnaire (GEQ) was developed in 1985 by Neil Widmeyer and his colleagues. It measures the cohesiveness of sports teams and relates closely to the material covered in Chapter 8. The Trait Sport Confidence Inventory (TSCI) and State Sport Confidence Inventory (SSCI) both measure confidence in sport and were developed by Robin Vealey in 1986. The TSCI assesses general level of sport confidence, whereas the SSCI is concerned with specific confidence prior to some type of performance or competition. The Leadership Scale for Sports (LSS), developed by Chella Chelladurai in 1980 relates closely to the material covered in Chapter 7. It assesses leadership style and types of behaviour used when coaching in sport.

These questionnaires are some of the most commonly used by sport psychology researchers, and in recent years they have yielded some interesting results which have helped us to understand and predict behaviour and performance in sport. Sometimes, practical sport psychologists also use these tests in their work with athletes, although views are mixed regarding the appropriateness and use of research instruments in an applied setting. Some individuals feel that the tests offer no help in their work with athletes, whereas others suggest that they provide useful information when assessing areas in which an athlete needs to improve.

A multitude of areas are open to investigation by the research sport psychologist. A few examples are listed below:

1.   The relationship between competitive anxiety and performance in different types of sport.
2.   How best to use rewards as a means of maintaining motivation during long hours of training.
3.   The different ways of using visualization to assist in the execution of sports skills.
4.   Techniques for building teamwork.
5.   Better and more efficient methods of assessing psychological skills related to exceptional athletic performance.

The results of research into these, and other areas is clearly of vital importance to the work of sport psychologists who are actually dealing directly with athletes and coaches. The skills and strategies which they teach to athletes will be firmly based on the results accumulated by the research sport psychologists.

Before reading on, pause for a moment and complete **Exercise 33**.

Exercise 33

Consider areas of research which interest you and which you feel would benefit your sport. What would you like a research sport psychologist to 'find out' if he or she decided to carry out a study in your sport?

Let us now return to an examination of the role of the practical sport psychologist. The following section describes different types of help which a sport psychologist can provide.

Psychological Support

For the purposes of this discussion, I am concerned with five different categories. Consider how important and how relevant each is to your own sport.

Performance Enhancement Training

Mental skills training is the most obvious, and visible, service which sport psychologists provide. As mentioned earlier, sport psychologists can teach athletes skills and strategies relating to motivation, anxiety and stress management, concentration, self-confidence and mental practice. These techniques are based on knowledge acquired through scientific research, and their implementation will vary according to the needs of the athlete and the demands of the sport. For a much deeper examination of these skills and how they can be used, you may wish to obtain a book entirely devoted to this area. One such book, *A Mental Game Plan* is dealt with in Further Reading.

Team Building and Social Development

Chapter 8 described a range of practical activities relating to the development of team spirit. Few athletes would deny the importance of team harmony and togetherness in achieving success. However, intra-group rivalries, personality clashes, poor communication skills and external pressures often combine to threaten the cohesion of a team and assistance is needed to identify problem areas and initiate appropriate methods of team-building.

Some sport psychologists have received extensive training and education in group dynamics, and have a special interest in team building and social development. They are able to implement group activities designed to improve communication channels within the team and hence develop greater team spirit and unity. For the past three years, I have been working with the England women's cricket team and of all the psychological aspects I have covered with them, they have informed me that the group development work has been the most beneficial. They report improved communication, increased confidence and greater team spirit having undergone a range of group activities involving evaluation discussions, problem-solving, strategical assessments, and the examination of individual roles within the squad.

Lifestyle Management Training

Many athletes lead very stressful lives. They travel a great deal, work to strict deadlines, are hounded by the media and are usually performing in achievement/competitive situations. Sport psychologists can therefore provide a valuable service in the form of lifestyle management training. Athletes can benefit from learning how to cope with daily hassles, how to manage their time effectively, and how to organize their lives so that their training time is as productive and efficient as possible. Although these areas are not directly performance-related, it seems reasonable to assume that if an athlete is generally relaxed and in control of life, then performances will improve.

More sport psychologists are now becoming involved in this type of work with athletes, and it is not only appropriate for top-level professional athletes. People who hold full-time jobs and play weekend sport often devote a substantial part of their lives to training and preparation for competition. This can lead to conflicts at home, increased levels of stress and generally decreased levels of satisfaction. Training in stress management, time management and interpersonal communication skills can therefore alleviate these problems, resulting in a much more satisfied and successful athlete.

Dealing with Injury

It is becoming increasingly common for sport psychologists to help an athlete deal with the psychological concerns experienced when an injury occurs. There are five areas in which help can be provided for an injured athlete. Each is briefly outlined below:

1. *Goal setting*. Athletes sometimes lose motivation when suffering a serious injury and the prospect of not playing for a long period of time is clearly disruptive to training schedules and progress goals. Goal setting is an excellent motivational technique but requires expertise to implement effectively. In consultation with the coach, a sport psychologist can assist the athlete in devising realistic goal targets which can sustain motivation and self-confidence throughout the rehabilitation period.
2. *Relaxation training*. Pain, anxiety, tension and boredom often accompany sports injury and lead to a variety of physical and mental stress responses. Instruction in appropriate relaxation training can assist the athlete in coping with these symptoms and hence contribute to a more tolerable period of acceptance and rehabilitation.
3. *Imagery/visualization*. Injury usually prevents practice and therefore presents an ideal opportunity for mental practice. This skill was covered in detail in Chapter 6. Its applications are numerous, but during injury-rehabilitation there are three particular uses which are worthwhile. First, the specific mental practice of technical skills. Second, the mental rehearsal of strategies and moves relating to competition. And third, imagery which prepares the athlete for the potential stress and pressure associated with returning to competition. The sport psychologist can help the athlete in devising imagery routines and setting up mental practice schedules.
4. *Self-talk*. Many injured athletes tend to dwell on rather negative and irrational thoughts. The sport psychologist can therefore teach the athlete how to develop more appropriate and positive thought patterns which concentrate on the anticipation of returning, rather than the dissappointment arising from injury.
5. *Social support*. Athletes often react very badly to injury and can become very depressed and dejected. A sport psychologist is well-placed as someone to whom the athlete can turn for a confidential chat or an emotional outburst. The sport psychologist

will provide appropriate support, encouragement and guidance on how to deal with the feelings resulting from the injury.

Coach Education

Sport psychologists are often employed as teachers on coach education programmes. It is important that coaches are aware of the mental skills and psychological strategies which their athletes are using so that they can show support and encourage the athlete to practise mental training regularly. Some coach education courses equip coaches with the skills to teach very basic mental training strategies to their athletes, such as using cue words and appropriate goal setting procedures. However, coaches should not overestimate the boundaries of their competence by attempting to teach athletes other, more advanced mental skills.

Many coach education programmes also cover aspects of team-building, communication skills and styles of leadership. Some sport psychologists, as mentioned earlier, have particular expertise in these areas and can assist coaches in developing their coaching behaviour and hence motivating their athletes. Much of the material covered in Chapter 7 is relevant and matches the content of some coach education courses.

In some circumstances, sport psychologists also work with coaches as they do with athletes. Coaches often experience excessive levels of competitive stress, periods of decreased confidence and their attentional requirements are sometimes excessive. They can therefore benefit from mental training education for themselves and can even develop their own individualized training programme which is clearly matched with the specific coaching demands of their sport.

Exercise 34

At the beginning of this section you were asked to consider how important and how relevant each of these five areas of psychological help is to your own sport. Pause now and make notes on how each of the five areas could be used in your sport.

1. Performance enhancement training.
2. Team building and social development.
3. Lifestyle management training.
4. Dealing with injury.
5. Coach education.

A Framework to Illustrate the Role of a Sport Psychologist

Having described the various types of aid which a sport psychologist can provide, this section will present a descriptive framework which illustrates the implementation of a consultancy service aimed at enhancing the performance of an individual athlete. The framework would equally apply to work with a team or squad and, with appropriate modifications, could also be used as the basis for work with a coach. The framework, shown in **Figure 43**, has six stages and assumes a long term involvement by the sport psychologist rather than an emergency, short-term consultancy.

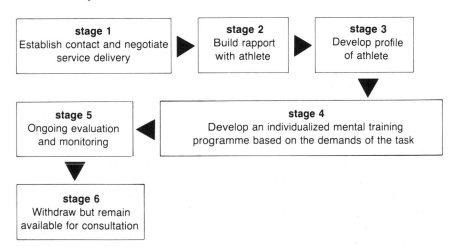

Fig 43   Framework to illustrate the role of the sport psychologist.

Stage 1: Contact and Negotiation

This first stage in the process involves the athlete and sport psychologist establishing contact and negotiating the type of aid which is desired and deemed appropriate. At this early point, the sport psychologist may feel unequipped in terms of expertise or experience to fulfil the required role, and therefore may refer the athlete to a colleague. Equally, the athlete may not feel that the sport psychologist is suitable and decide to look elsewhere for assistance. If, however, there is mutual agreement between athlete and sport psychologist, stage 2 commences . . .

Stage 2: Building Rapport

This stage is vital if the sport psychologist is to be effective. There must be mutual trust and respect between both individuals, and the athlete must feel free to confide in the sport psychologist. It should be accepted that the sport psychologist is an addition, rather than a replacement to the coaching staff. Likewise, it is the responsibility of the sport psychologist to become involved in the athlete's training and competition, rather than always operating from an office. Some of the most successful sport psychology interventions have occurred in the gymnasium or out on the field during practice where the mental skills can be seen as being relevant, meaningful and useful.

Stage 3: Individudal Profiling

When a rapport between athlete and sport psychologist has been established, a profiling procedure can begin in a non-threatening and often enjoyable manner. The sport psychologist needs to identify the various sport-related psychological strengths and weaknesses of the athlete before being able to effectively develop a training programme. This is similar to fitness testing prior to the prescription of an exercise, or strength training programme for an athlete.

Sport psychologists use a variety of methods for obtaining information relating to this sport-related psychological profile. Some use standard questionnaires of the type described earlier (eg, SCAT, CSAI-2, SPSQ and TSCI) whereas others prefer to spend time interviewing the athlete. Observing the athlete in competition is a frequently used technique and, of course, information from the coach is often useful. It is usual to use a combination of these methods in an attempt to obtain as much information as possible, thereby making the job of developing an appropriate training programme much easier.

Stage 4: Individualized Mental Training Programme

Having formulated a profile of the athlete, it is necessary to examine the particular demands of the task at hand. The psychological requirements of checking in ice hockey are quite different from those of putting in golf. Likewise, the pre-competition routines of gymnasts will differ from those of marathon runners. Therefore, the development of an individualized mental training programme will depend on a combination of the athlete profile and the demands of the sport. The outcome of this may be a training programme orientated mostly towards relaxation and visualization exercises, as opposed to another which may focus almost entirely on positive thinking and self-talk.

Stage 5: Continuous Evaluation

Whilst the mental training programme is being implemented, its effectiveness must be monitored closely by the sport psychologist who will perhaps discuss aspects of performance improvement with the coach. Periodically, adjustments will be made to the programme and skills may be progressively developed as the athlete's mental training ability improves. Occasionally, the sport psychologist is needed to intervene when a perceived problem occurs such as an injury, a performance slump, or a conflict between two athletes on a team. This may expose the need for additional skills to be included in the mental training programme, and a temporary return to Stage 4 may be necessary.

Stage 6: Withdrawal

As the athlete learns more about mental skills training and becomes more experienced at employing the techniques successfully, the sport psychologist will become less involved. The athlete should not be dependent on the services of a sport psychologist but rather develop the skills associated with self-control, and then take personal responsibility for their implementation. Eventually, the sport psychologist can then withdraw and begin working with other athletes. Nevertheless, future availability is an important option for the athlete, so that the sport psychologist can be consulted if necessary.

Ethical Considerations

To conclude this chapter, it is important to examine briefly the ethical considerations concerning practising sport psychologists. Sport psychology associations around the world have codes of conduct which are designed to guide the professional behaviour of their practising members. Some codes are long and extensive, but they are each similar in a number of areas. Three of these areas are briefly described below and illustrate the general philosophy adopted by most practising sport psychologists when working with athletes and teams, or conducting research studies.

The Welfare of the Athlete

A sport psychologist's primary concern is for the welfare of the athlete. Although the service being delivered may be predominantly orientated towards performance enhancement, this must not be at the expense of the psychological and emotional health of the athlete. In other words, a happy athlete is the sport psychologist's most important goal. Having said this, however, one could argue that a happy athlete is more likely to become a successful athlete and this is obviously a desirable outcome.

Understanding Competence

Sport psychologists are expected to recognize the boundaries and limitations of their own competence. They are advised not to operate beyond these boundaries, and are encouraged to refer athletes or coaches to colleagues who are more appropriately qualified and experienced, should the need arise.

Confidentiality

Sport psychologists, like any other other type of psychologist, are expected to maintain confidentiality when working with athletes and coaches. Information gleaned from interviews or from psychological questionnaires should not be disclosed to anyone other than the person involved, unless permission is formally granted. This is essential in order to maintain the integrity of the sport psychologist who clearly needs honesty and openness when involved in a consultation.

Conclusion

The role of the sport psychologist has developed rapidly over the last decade, and demand for sport psychology aid continues to grow. The sport psychologist can fulfil a number of different roles in performance enhancement training, team building and social development, lifestyle management training, dealing with injury, and coach education. In each of these areas the ethical considerations of athlete welfare, understanding competence and confidentiality are of the utmost importance and should frame the mode of operation employed by the sport psychologist.

Several countries, including Britain, Canada and America now have established registers containing the names of individuals who have met the professional requirements of a sport psychologist. Each of these registers also has an accompanying code of conduct, elaborating on the three areas mentioned above. The process by which an individual becomes accredited is a carefully considered one. Documentary evidence of academic qualifications is required and individuals are expected to have demonstrated expertise in sport psychology in the form of research publications and/or consultancy experience with athletes.

CHAPTER TWELVE

Conclusions and Recommendations

Dr Stephen J. Bull

At the end of Chapter 1 I suggested that your personal definition of sport psychology would be a much broader one than psyching up athletes or helping athletes handle the pressure of competition. Having read the preceding chapters I am hopeful that this is now the case. Hopefully, the previous 10 chapters have demonstrated the extent of knowledge currently present in the discipline of sport psychology. Also remember that this book is only focusing on the psychology of competitive sport. Books of equal size could have been written on the psychology of exercise, fitness and motor skill development, etc, all of which are considered aspects of 'sport psychology'.

Understanding the psychological processes associated with performance in competitive sport is imperative for those wishing to improve their own performance potential, and/or that of others. The practical exercises which appear throughout this book have been included to facilitate this understanding although they, and the book as a whole, are merely a starting point. Sport psychology does not execute miracles and will not transform an athlete with average ability into a Daley Thompson.

Sport psychology needs continued and consistent attention and should be an important element in the training of athletes, coaches, referees, teachers and even sport administrators. Given this degree of consideration, sport psychology does have the potential to significantly improve the performance and satisfaction of athletes, coaches and others associated with competitive sport and physical activity. It can also assist in promoting acceptable sporting behaviour. It can enable athletes to perform to the best of their ability. It can help a coach get the best out of the athletes or team. It can contribute to increased levels of enjoyment by children participating in competitive sport. It can prevent individuals becoming stale, burnt out and abandoning the sport. It can assist athletes recovering from injury, and it can contribute to the effective management of an athlete's lifestyle.

You have probably found that some chapters in the book have

been more useful and interesting to you than others. This is to be expected, given the wide-ranging demands of different sports as well as the contrasting personalities of those who compete in them. Before reading on, take some time and begin **Exercise 35** which will help you to formulate action plans regarding the most useful points you can utilize having read this book.

Exercise 35

1. Briefly review the preceding chapters and identify three practical action points which you feel you could implement. Write these three points in your notebook.
2. Now think carefully about what specific changes you need to make in order to achieve the desired outcomes relating to these action points.
3. Over the coming month, monitor your progress in acting on these changes and assess the degree to which you achieve your aims.
4. At the end of the month, evaluate the success of your action plans.
5. For the following month, repeat the process by either creating a new set of action plans or by re-focusing on the existing ones if more work needs to be done.

Further Reading

For those readers who may wish to pursue their knowledge of sport psychology further, I have selected five books which should be of interest. Each of the books is directly related to the material to which you have been introduced in this book. They are well written and employ a practical style enabling you to utilize the information effectively in the sporting context.

Motivation: Implications for Coaching and Teaching A.V. Carron, 1984. Available from Spodym Publishers (address at end of chapter).

This book follows directly from the chapter on motivation by Dr Richard Cox. It is packed with practical suggestions and implications for both coaches and physical education teachers. The book examines a wide range of motivational techniques such as using token rewards, goal setting, social reinforcement, leadership behaviour, and competition. It analyses the influence of intrinsic interest, incentive motivation, self-confidence, anxiety, the need for achievement and focus of attention. Each chapter consists of a number of propositions, a number of practical implications, a summary and a list of suggested related readings. It is an ideal handbook for those wishing to promote or maintain the motivation of competitive athletes, recreational athletes or individuals learning sports skills for the first time.

A Mental Game Plan: A Training Program for all Sports J.G. Albinson and S.J. Bull, 1988. Available from Spodym Publishers (address at end of chapter).

This mental training workbook is a detailed elaboration of the area covered briefly by Brian Miller in his chapter on mental preparation for competition. The book contains an abundance of practical exercises, is written for both coaches and athletes, and provides examples of how to implement mental training exercises throughout. There are chapters devoted to goal setting, arousal management, visualization, concentration, positive thinking, stress management, energizing and preparation routines. The final section of the book contains the scripts for a number of practical relaxation exercises which could be used for both sport-related and non-sport-related stress management. This book is well suited to athletes and/or coaches wishing to develop a systematic individualized mental training programme as a means of enhancing performance potential.

Team Spirit J. Syer, 1986. Available from The Sporting Bodymind (address at end of chapter).

If you enjoyed reading John Syer's chapter on team building and wish to learn more about the area, then this book is highly recommended. Written by John himself, it extensively covers such areas as morale, conflict, conformity, relationships, communication, motivation, confidence and stress. It is backed by a wealth of practical experience in the area of team building and will be of interest to individuals in business, as well as coaches of team games and sports groups. The book is not as practically structured as the previous two described, but nevertheless contains plenty of useful advice and suggestions.

Parenting Your Superstar R.J. Rotella and L.K. Bunker, 1987. Available from Human Kinetics Publishers (address at end of chapter).

This book clearly follows on from the chapter contributed by Misia Gervis on children in sport. It is designed to assist parents in helping their child get the most out of sports. It is a practical book which aims to guide you through the pleasures and perils of raising a child athlete. The book explains how to encourage a child's interest in sport, and how to balance the demands of sport

Sport psychology will not transform an athlete with average ability into a Daley Thompson.

with the needs of a family. There are very useful sections on how parents can help a child set realistic goals and how they can help their child become more confident and secure.

Towards the end of the book there are important sections on effective practice sessions, preventing injuries, competition and nutrition, organized youth sports, the benefits of sports participation, and sport and personal development. This book is highly recommended to parents who are concerned about providing the appropriate sport experience for their children so that they will gain maximum enjoyment and satisfaction.

Coaches Guide to Sport Psychology R. Martens, 1987. Available from Human Kinetics Publishers (address at end of chapter).

There are three sections in this excellent workbook written by one of the pioneers of international sport psychology, Dr Rainer Martens. Section 1 is called 'Psychological perspectives' and includes chapters on the philosophy of coaching and motivation. Section 2, covering psychological skills for coaches, contains chapters on leadership and communication. Section 3 is related to athlete psychological skills and covers imagery, stress management, concentration, self-confidence and goal setting. The style of the book is very easy-to-read and there are many exercises and guidelines which will be of great benefit to coaches wishing to understand the practical relevance of sport psychology. The book is used as one of the texts in the American Coaching Effectiveness Program, Level 2, Sport Science Curriculum.

A *Sport Psychology Study Guide* is also used on this course which is written to help coaches apply the psychological information to their own coaching programmes. Further information about the American Coaching Effectiveness Program can be obtained by writing to the address listed at the end of this chapter.

In Britain, similar courses to those of the American Coaching Effectiveness Program (ACEP) are run by the National Coaching Foundation (NCF). The address for the NCF is listed at the end of this chapter. Of particular interest to the reader would be the courses and workshops which cover such areas as mental preparation for performance, understanding and improving skill, motivating your athlete, mental training, children and competitive sport, working with teams, and communication.

Details of these, and other, sport psychology courses can be obtained by contacting the NCF headquarters. In conjunction with the British Association of Sports Sciences, the NCF has also produced a series of sports science monographs, one of which is entitled *Mental Training in Sport: An Overview*. Although this monograph is not written in the practical style emphasized throughout this book, it may be of interest to those readers who wish to investigate the theoretical aspects of sport psychology in more detail.

Final Recommendations to Different Types of Reader

To conclude this chapter, and the book, a number of recommendations are now made. These recommendations vary according to your involvement in competitive sport and are designed to assist you in using your sport psychology knowledge productively.

Athletes

1. With the help of your coach and, if possible, a sport psychologist, identify your strengths and weaknesses regarding the mental side of sport performance. A mental training workbook will also help you to do this.
2. Develop an individualized mental training programme with the help of your coach, a mental training workbook and, if possible, a sport psychologist.
3. Periodically re-read the chapters in this book which are most relevant to you. These may include the chapters on motivation, stress and anxiety, and mental preparation for competition.

Coaches

1. Attend training courses and workshops in sport psychology to update your knowledge in the latest techniques which have been developed to assist athletes in competition.
2. Assess your own coaching style and evaluate your skills in motivating athletes, communicating, and fostering team spirit among the groups of performers with whom you work.
3. Periodically re-read the chapters in this book which are most relevant to you. These may include the chapters on motivation, aggression, coach–athlete relationships, team building, children in sport and burnout.

Parents

1.   Emphasise enjoyment as a major priority in your child's sporting involvement.
2.   Always consider your child's long-term development.
3.   Periodically re-read the chapters in this book which are most relevant to you. These may include the chapters on interpreting success and failure, children in sport and burnout.

Referees

1.   Use some of the mental skills identified in this book for your own performance preparation.
2.   Attend stress management workshops to develop your coping skills.
3.   Periodically re-read the chapters in this book which are most relevant to you. These may include the chapters on stress and anxiety, mental preparation for competition and burnout.

Potential Sport Psychologists

1.   Get plenty of experience as a performer and a coach.
2.   Complete a first degree in either psychology, sports science, physical education or a related subject. Then register for a higher degree in a sport psychology-related subject.
3.   Periodically re-read the chapter in this book on the role of the sport psychologist, and also begin reading academic sport psychology texts such as those listed below:

Carron, A.V. (1988), *Group Dynamics in Sport*, (Eastbourne: Spodym).
Cox, R.H. (1990), *Sport Psychology: Concepts and Applications*, (Dubuque, IA: Wm.C. Brown).
Cratty, B.J. (1989), *Psychology in Contemporary Sport*, 3rd Edition, (Englewood Cliffs, NJ: Prentice-Hall).
Gill, D. (1986), *Psychological Dynamics of Sport*, (Champaign, IL: Human Kinetics).
Williams, J. (1986), *Applied Sport Psychology: Personal growth to peak performance*, (Palo Alto, CA: Mayfield).

List of Addressess

Spodym Publishers
102, Anderida Road,
Eastbourne,
East Sussex,
BN22 0QD,
England.

Ocean House,
2649 Heron Street
Victoria
British Columbia,
V8R 5Z9,
Canada.

The Sporting Bodymind
18 Kemplay Road,
London,
NW3 1SY,
England.

P.O. Box 224,
Birmingham,
Michigan, 48012,
USA.

Human Kinetics Publishers
P.O. Box 18,
Rawdon,
Leeds,
LS19 6TG,
England.

Box 5076,
Champaign,
Illinois, 61825,
USA.

*American Coaching
  Effectiveness Program*
Box 5076,
Champaign,
Illinois, 61825,
USA.

National Coaching Foundation
4 College Close,
Beckett Park,
Leeds,
LS6 3QH,
England.

Glossary

Aggression: Any behaviour intended to harm another individual by physical or verbal means.

Anxiety: The results of an individual's negative appraisal of his/her ability to meet the demands of a specific situation.

Athlete: An individual who actively participates in competitive sport.

Attributions: Perceived reasons or causes given for a particular event or outcome, such as losing a competition.

Behavioural contract: The development of a written agreement between two individuals (usually the athlete and coach) expressing the desired behaviour changes and consequences of those changes.

Centering: A technique for controlling arousal either before, or during, competition.

Coach education: Aid or support provided by sport psychologists, designed to teach coaches the fundamentals of mental skills training.

Cognitive anxiety: The mental elements of anxiety, such as negative expectations and worry.

Competitive state anxiety: Anxiety experienced at a specific point in time in relation to a specific competition.

Competitive stress: Feelings of anxiety and/or discomfort associated with competition.

Competitive trait anxiety: A predisposition to experience anxiety in competitive situations.

Confluence: Sense of belonging experienced by each member of a synergistic team.

Corrective feedback: Comments made to an athlete by a person that indicate why the athlete's performance was good, and precisely how that performance could be improved.

Depersonalization: A state in which relationships with others are perceived as more negative and antagonistic than previously.

Dropout: When an individual discontinues an activity for reasons which may, or may not, be related to burnout.

Ego goal: When the goal set as the criterion for success is winning, and being better than others.

Energizing: A technique for increasing arousal either before, or during, competition.

Ethical considerations: Factors relating to the appropriateness of a sport psychologist's method or conduct.

External motivation: Motivation maintained through external means.

Goal aggression: Aggressive acts that have harm as the primary aim; aggression performed as an end in itself.

Goal setting: A process of setting targets as a means of developing motivation and directing appropriate attentional focus.

Individual profiling: A technique used by sport psychologists to identify the sport-related psychological strengths and weaknesses of an athlete.

Instrumental aggression: Aggressive acts that are performed to achieve a non-aggressive goal; aggression performed as a means to an end.

Intrinsic motivation: Motivation maintained through internal means.

Kinaesthesis: The information we receive from our joints concerning their state of tension.

Learned helplessness: A negative emotional, cognitive and behavioural state which leads to withdrawal from a situation of failure.

Lifestyle management training: Aid or support provided by sport psychologists, designed to help an athlete cope with stress, manage time and organise life to allow for optimum performance potential.

Locus of causality: The cause for behaviour – located within the individual (internal) or outside the individual (external).

Mastery goal: When the goal set as the criterion for success is self-improvement and mastery of the task.

Mental exhaustion: A state of emotional and cognitive fatigue which develops over time in response to stress.

Mental training programme: A systematically developed programme of training designed to improve an athlete's ability to cope with the psychological demands of competitive sport.

Neutral statements: Statements of fact that contain neither value judgements nor corrective information. They usually begin with 'I see' or 'I notice'.

Overtraining: Involvement in activity which is excessive relative to the individual's ability to adapt to, and recover from, the demands.

Participation motives: The reasons people take part in any particular activity.

Performance enhancement training: Aid or support provided by sport psychologists, designed to improve an athlete's performance potential.

Performance segmenting: A technique for enabling consistency in performance by being adequately prepared during the pre-competition phase.

Physical burnout: A state of continuous physical fatigue and tiredness which requires more brief periods of rest to recover.

Pre-event focusing: A technique which encourages an athlete to focus on process rather than outcome during a competition.

Psychological burnout: Feelings of mental exhaustion, depersonalization and reduced personal accomplishment.

Primary feedback: The information we receive directly from taking part in an activity.

Primary motivation: The positive or negative effects of taking part in the activity itself.

Proprioception: The information we receive from our joints concerning their position and orientation.

Register: A list of accredited sport psychology professionals who have met the necessary criteria as laid down by a national sport psychology association.

Reinforcer: Anything that happens after a particular behaviour that changes the probability of the same behaviour occurring again.

Response prevention: The development of a specific plan to anticipate potential problem situations, and the appropriate response to these situations if they occur.

Secondary feedback: The information we are given about a performance in an activity which does not derive from the activity itself.

Secondary motivation: The positive or negative effects of any source of influence other than the activity itself.

Self-confidence: An individual's positive perception of his/her ability to meet the demands of a specific task in a specific situation.

Self-control: The placing of primary responsibility for behaviour change on the individual self.

Self-esteem: How one feels about oneself in relation to others.

Somatic anxiety: The individual's perception of his/her physiological symptoms of anxiety.

Sport psychologist: An individual who is a qualified professional in the area of sport psychology.

Stress: A stimulus in the form of demands placed upon the individual by the environment.

Synergy: The strength, ability and creativity of a whole team which is greater than the sum of the individual members.

Team building: A type of service delivery, provided by sport psychologists, designed to develop the team spirit of a sports group.

Value-laden feedback: Comments made to an athlete by a person that indicate what the person thinks emotionally about the athlete's performance – e g, 'good shot' or 'well done'.

Vicarious aggression: The learning of aggressive responses by simply viewing another person acting aggressively.

Index